Safe at Home!

BASEBALL AND OUR PILGRIMAGE HOME

michael **FOX**

m•agine!

Dedicated to

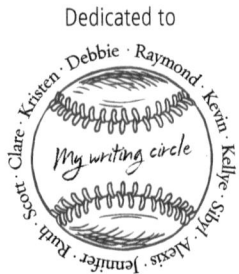

Copyright © 2019 by Michael Fox

Safe at Home! Baseball and Our Pilgrimage Home

by Michael Fox

m•agine!

407 Myrtle Drive • Farmerville, LA 71241

Printed in the United States of America

ISBN 978-0-359-82032-0

All rights reserved solely by the author. The author guarantees all contents are original and do not infringe upon the legal rights of any other person or work. No part of this book may be reproduced in any form without the permission of the author. The views expressed in this book are not necessarily those of the publisher.

Scripture taken from the

NEW AMERICAN STANDARD BIBLE.

Copyright © 1960, 1962, 1963, 1968, 1971, 1972, 1973, 1975, 1977, 1995

by The Lockman Foundation. Used by permission.

Cover image(s) used under license from Shutterstock.com.

Safe at Home!

WARM-UP:
THE THIRD BASE COACH
9

THE FIRST:
"PLAY BALL!"
15

THE SECOND:
THE SOUL OF THE GAME
37

THE THIRD:
TIME AND SPACE
57

THE FOURTH:
GREEN CATHEDRALS
85

THE FIFTH:
6 + 4 + 3 = 2
109

THE SIXTH:
CARDS AND GIANTS
135

THE SEVENTH:
STITCHES
151

THE EIGHTH:
STORYTELLERS
165

THE NINTH:
SAFE AT HOME
185

EXTRA INNINGS:
"GOING DEEP!"
203

:
GRATITUDE
213

WARM-UP:

THE THIRD BASE COACH

You see, you spend a good piece of your life gripping a baseball,

and in the end it turns out

that it was the other way around all the time.

Jim Bouton

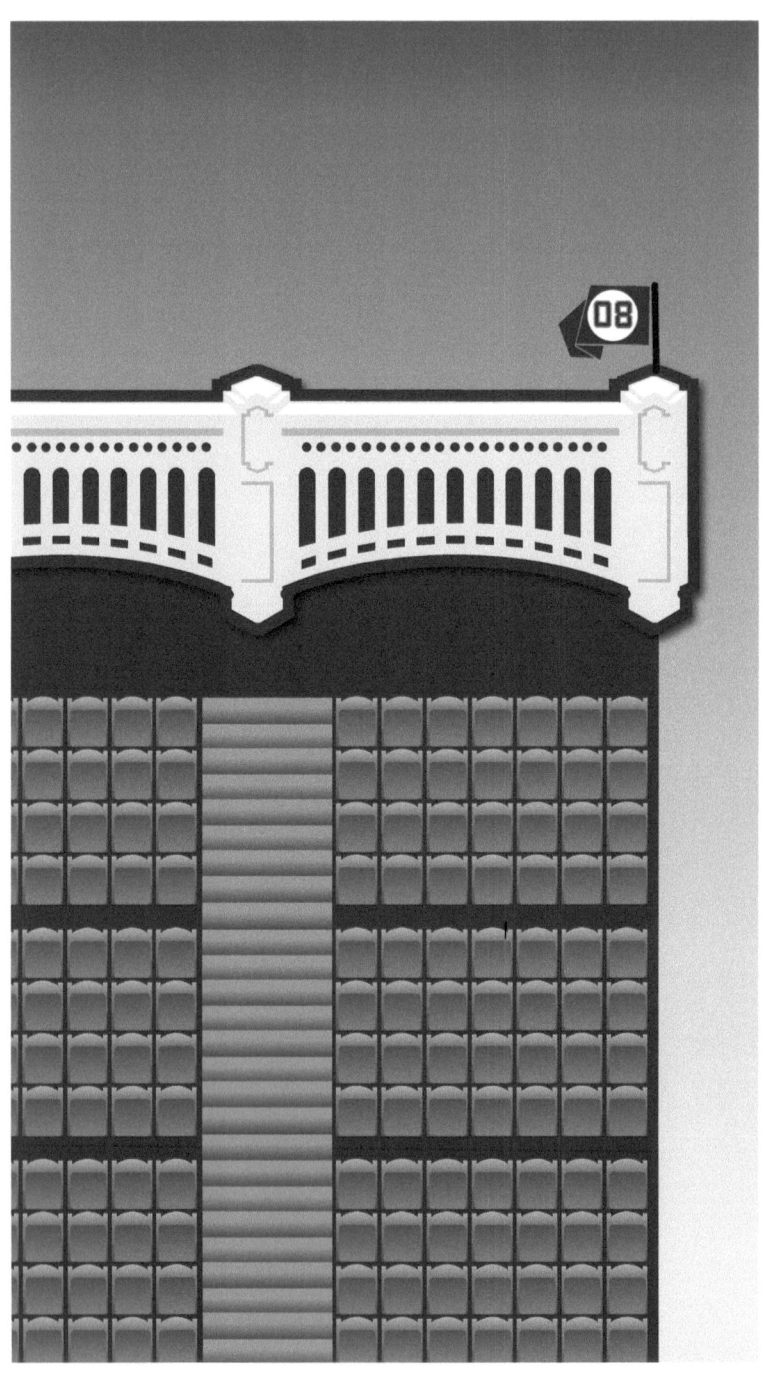

WARM-UP:

THE THIRD BASE COACH

The collected essays within this book were written over a ten-year period. I intentionally chose not to update details that might have changed through intervening years. The following introduction, for example, was written prior to the Dodgers' reemerrgence in the World Series in 2017. Finally.

At last count, the Los Angeles Dodgers employed fourteen coaches. Fourteen. That's just about one coach for every three players. Fourteen. That's just a handful more than the number of games by which they lost the pennant last year. Fourteen. That's about half as many years since they last appeared in the World Series. Fourteen. That's a lot of coaches.

SAFE AT HOME!

As a coach in the fields of life and ministry and business, I feel a particular affinity toward the third base coach.

The third base coach has one primary responsibility: get the base runner safely home. Toward this end, he is in constant communication with the base runner. Most of it is non-verbal communication; in fact, to the casual observer, the third base coach appears to be doing something akin to the chicken dance in his box on the field. The third base coach often has to decide in a moment whether to hold the runner at third or to wave him home. The third base coach—in that singular moment—must respect the base runner's athletic prowess and his competitive desire to get home, but, when necessary, have the temerity to give him the stop sign.

The third base coach can see what the runner can't see as he blindly runs the bases toward home. The third base coach sees the right fielder play the carom off the wall. He watches as the fielder digs the ball out of his glove. Did he handle it cleanly? He looks to see where the fielder is throwing the ball: will he throw to third?... will he try to throw directly to the plate?... will he throw to a cut-off man, who will in turn fire the ball to third or home?... or will the fielder concede the base and merely toss the ball back to the pitcher? Is the ball thrown with precision? I've seen games won and lost on the decision of the third base coach.

I've witnessed third base coaches and players, though on the same team, go after each other following a busted play. Sometimes they square off toe-to-toe on the field; sometimes they wait until they return to the dugout. Sometimes the coach is calming the competitive passion of the player; sometimes he's calling him forth—challenging his potential, so that next time the player won't be called out at home.

I often evaluate my work using the third base coach as a metaphor. I point my charges in the direction of home. I do my best to see what they cannot see. And sometimes, I have to call them forth. In my work, home is not on a diamond. Typically, home is either a space where their goals are fulfilled or where they might live in alignment with their values. A coach is more than a cheerleader. The best coaches will occasionally risk themselves or the relationship itself on behalf of their clients, calling them forth so they won't be called out.

At the risk of sounding clichéd, I like to think of Jesus as a third base coach, pointing people home. Toward that end, he calls his people out. In fact, that's the very meaning of the Greek word translated church. The church is comprised of those who have been called out. But mightn't it be possible we've missed the import of that word? A Christ follower is not simply called out to isolation and inactivity. He is called out in order to be called forth. Called forth to priesthood. Called forth to mission. And often, Jesus finds it necessary to call forth his people to the fullest extension of their abilities. Called forth so as to be called safe. At home.

But, what if you aren't a person of faith? What if—and, I confess I find this statement so unlikely as to be amusing—you don't care about baseball? If you read through to the end, you will find value.

SAFE AT HOME!

THE FIRST:
"PLAY BALL!"

I don't want to play golf.

When I hit a ball, I want someone else to go chase it.

Rogers Hornsby

THE FIRST:

"PLAY BALL!"

There is an element of the Divine in baseball. In the Old Testament, the word holy is often contrasted with the word profane, or common. With respect to the meat offered in sacrifice, the LORD told Moses, "And everyone who eats it will bear his iniquity, for he has profaned [or, made common] the holy thing of the LORD..." (Leviticus 19:8). Holy, uncommon. Wholly uncommon.

And now for something completely different...the game of baseball is wholly uncommon among outdoor team games; consider:

Baseball can't be played in inclement weather. Baseball respects, and is perfectly placed within, the seasons of the year: it begins in spring when all things are new; it endures the long, intense days of summer; it bids farewell with the lengthening shadows and turning leaves of autumn.

Baseball, consistent with its pastoral character, is played in a park. The first modern baseball game was befittingly played at Elysian Fields in Hoboken, New Jersey. In Greek mythology, the Elysian Fields was the final resting place of the heroic and virtuous. Early Church Fathers adopted the term Elysian Fields as a synonym for Paradise.

Baseball is played on a field within the park. A baseball field features a compelling tension between the symmetrical and the irregular. Every field features a circle (the pitcher's mound) within a diamond (the base path) within a cropped circle (the infield), the placement of which are prescribed in the rule book with an engineer's precision. In contrast, the walls of the outfield—while subject to prescribed minimum and maximum distances from home plate—may differ from one field to another. One field may be shallow, a hitter's park, while another may be deep, a pitcher's park; the walls of one field may form a fluid curve from left to right, while another may be distinguished by sharp, random angles. The left and right field foul lines—which, in spite of the misnomer, mark fair territory—run the depth of the field at a right angle from home plate, where they ultimately meet the foul poles and where the boundaries of the field turn heavenward and, in effect, know no bounds.

Baseball, incidentally, may be the only game where players succeed by hitting the ball out of the park—they are rewarded by hitting the ball beyond the bounds of the field. And, by the way, in what other team game does the defense have the ball?

BASEBALL AND OUR PILGRIMAGE HOME

Baseball's symmetry on the field has its counterpart in the rules of the game. There are three strikes, three outs, three sets of three for a total of nine innings, nine players on the field. And only in baseball is there the hope of perfection, when a pitcher gets three up and three down in each of nine innings.

Baseball's objective is to leave home and to return home safely. Football's objective, by contrast, is to make incursion into enemy territory—perhaps by throwing a bomb, often against the defensive blitz—and crossing into the opponent's end zone. Baseball's home plate, not home base—unlike the geometrically simple squares, circles and diamonds of the outlying field—is a familiar pentagon that recalls a child's stick drawing of home. Home plate, in a striking display of ecumenical fellowship, is shared by both opposing teams.

Baseball is timeless. There is no clock in baseball; in fact, as if in spite of the clock and time itself, the game of baseball moves around the bases counterclockwise. A baseball game could, in theory, extend endlessly into extra innings. Although the uninitiated regard baseball as a slow game, at any given moment there are numerous areas of activity on the field, in the dugout, in the bullpen.

Baseball is a narrative. Within the rigid structure of the playing field and the rule book, each game is an unfolding and unanticipated, sometimes indeed chaotic, drama of redemption—of reconciliation—a Homeresque story of coming home to the embrace of family. The individual and the team, or community. Law and grace. Hits and misses. Runs and errors. Players enter and leave the story, sometimes only to sacrifice themselves for the benefit of the team, never to return. And only baseball chronicles each game so methodically that the game's narrative can be read and recounted, unedited, from the scorecard.

Baseball. A timeless narrative of reconciliation and coming home. To wonder-filled readers of scripture, it's a familiar theme.

Granted, you may sense no connection with the game of baseball. Might there be, then, another personal metaphor that connects you with the Divine Narrative of reconciliation and coming home found in scripture? § What can you do to deepen your appreciation, your sense of wonder, around the Divine Narrative of scripture?

On Monday and Tuesday, September 15th and 16th of 2008, I joined my nephews—Kevin from Midland, Texas, along with his then three-year old son Andrew, and Daniel from Los Angeles, California—at old Yankee Stadium in New York. On Tuesday morning, Daniel returned to law school at UCLA; his seat was filled for the second game by a young friend from Auburn, Jackson Tate. (An extraordinary story for another time.) We converged upon the Bronx for two games of the final week in the life of the grand dame of ballparks before her demise that winter. We watched the White Sox, led by Ken Griffey Jr., engage the Yankees, captained by Derek Jeter.

BASEBALL AND OUR PILGRIMAGE HOME

A quarter century before, when they were about five and three, I took Kevin and Daniel to their first Major League Baseball game—a magical evening at Chavez Ravine where the Dodgers hosted the Mets. Years later, here I was accompanying Kevin and Daniel to a ballgame, but this time it was to carry Andrew, yet another generation, to his first game—a world away from Dodgers Stadium in The House that Ruth Built.

On Monday night, we sat some twenty rows up an imagined extension of the first-base line into the stands behind home plate. Magnificent. On Tuesday night, however, we chose to experience the game in the stadium's right field stands, home to the legendary Bleacher Creatures, led by Bald Vinny Milano. Epic.

I first learned of the Bleacher Creatures from my older brother Kevin who, for a time, worked in New York City. He told me stories of sitting in the right field bleachers, inaccessible to the primary concourse of the stadium. Occasionally, fans from the top tier of the stadium would lean precipitously over the rail and peer down into the crowded bleachers below, drawn by the cheers and jeers of the boisterous fans in the "cheap seats" of right field. In unison, Kevin recalled, the Bleacher Creatures would turn to the curious, upper deck fans and yell, "Jump!"

The Bleacher Creatures are best known for Roll Call in the top of the first inning of every home game. As the Yankees' starting pitcher prepares to throw the first pitch, everyone in the right field bleachers stands and begins to clap; after the first pitch is thrown, Bald Vinny quiets the crowd and Roll Call begins. The Bleacher Creatures, once again in unison, chant the names of the Yankees fielders, one by one, beginning with team captain, Derek Jeter. The chant continues until each player—save for the pitcher and catcher—in turn, doffs his cap, takes a bow, waves his hand, salutes, or otherwise acknowledges the denizens of right field. No one among the fans outside of the Bleacher Creatures encroaches upon this tradition; Roll Call is the proprietary role of the right field pavilion.

The remarkable thing about Roll Call is the intimate moment when the heroes of the game turn and acknowledge the presence of the anonymous fans in the stands. It's all the more remarkable in an age—unlike a bygone era—when players scarcely ever acknowledge the presence of the "huge crowd of witnesses" surrounding them.

Which leads to my point.

As memorable as it was to be a part of Roll Call that Tuesday night in the Bronx, I can only imagine what it must be like to be on the other end of the fun—to be on the field of play and to hear the passionate and persistent call of your name by those gathered in the stands. In a nation of three hundred million people, less than a thousand play Major League Baseball at any given time. Only twenty-five of those play for the Yankees; and only a third of those regularly take the field at the outset of the game and hear their names chanted from the right field pavilion.

Followers of Jesus, however, can have a sense of being on the field for Roll Call. The anonymous author of Hebrews penned a Roll Call

BASEBALL AND OUR PILGRIMAGE HOME

in chapter 11—a Roll Call of faithful men and women who had once run the track on the stadium floor. These heroes, having finished their course, have retired to the stands. Today, they are among the "huge crowd of witnesses" who now cheer us on. Can you hear them calling you out... calling you forth...calling you by name?

What specific words of encouragement do you need to hear from the "huge crowd of witnesses" to keep you running with faithfulness and endurance? § If you were to finish your race and take your place in the stands right now, based on your experience, what would you desire to convey to the current runners? Why wait until you're in the stands?

Regrettably, I can't remember the first major league baseball game I attended; in fact, I can't remember—forgive my errant grammar—having ever *not* visited beautiful Dodger Stadium in Chavez Ravine, overlooking the Los Angeles skyline, a couple of times a year. But if others' memory can be compared to a Rembrandt portrait of striking, near photographic, detail, then my memory can be compared, perhaps kindly, as a Monet Impressionistic landscape...

I recall moments.

Willie Mays patrolling center field...Willie Stargell hitting a home run over the right field pavilion... Passing Casey Stengel and

Babe Herman in a corridor following an Old-Timers' Game... Watching Dizzy Dean enter the press box... My first ball game out of town at San Francisco's Candlestick Park... Taking Kevin and Daniel—and, later, Andrew—to their first ball games. Cal Ripken hitting a home run to left field in old Yankees Stadium... Singing *Take Me Out to the Ballgame* at Chicago's Wrigley Field and *Sweet Caroline* at Boston's Fenway Park... The Angels' Devon White stealing second, then third, then home... Watching the Cubs play the Dodgers from Lew Wasserman's dugout seats at Dodgers Stadium... A congratulatory message on the scoreboard from the Brooklyn Dodgers' Zach Wheat to the Los Angeles Dodgers' Willie Davis... A slender slugger from USC named Mark McGwire playing in the 1984 Los Angeles Olympics... Fernando Valenzuela and Nolan Ryan squaring off in a pitching duel... Hearing the majestic voice of the late Bob Shepard announce the line-ups at Yankees Stadium... Vin Scully, period.

Just moments. Impressions. So...

What experiences, what impressions, what defining moments, what learnings, do you need to journal for your sake and for the sake of your descendants? § All of this makes me grateful that the Apostle John, at nearly a century old, relented and wrote the gospel that bears his name. Ask me, if you're curious. § Whether you paint your memories after the style of Rembrandt or Monet, I encourage you to put the brush to canvas, the pen to paper, the memory to posterity.

BASEBALL AND OUR PILGRIMAGE HOME

I've stood atop The Green Monster of Boston's Fenway Park. I've sat among the Bleacher Creatures in the right field grandstand of New York's old Yankee Stadium. I've witnessed a ball fly over the ivy-covered outfield walls of Chicago's Wrigley Field. I've walked through the tunnel and onto the field of Abner Doubleday Field in Cooperstown, New York, the fabled—that is to say, not the actual—birthplace of baseball. It isn't difficult for me to imagine layers of ghostly players from multiple eras, batting the ball, running to first, chasing a fly. These venerable ballparks are timeless spaces, playing host to men playing a boys' game, without the intrusion of a clock.

Granted, you can look about and find timepieces even in the confines of an ancient baseball park. A clock on the scoreboard announces the local time; an analog clock in the dugout is protected by a cage from an errant foul ball; a watch might be worn by a fan, or even by at least one big league manager—curious, indeed (although, the way his team is currently playing, he might be counting the minutes until he can leave the park). A timepiece in a baseball park, however, has no impact upon the game; as a matter of fact, a timepiece in a baseball park is but a regrettable reminder that, outside this timeless space, time continues its oppressive reign.

The timelessness of baseball, especially as played within the embrace of the old parks, reflects the timelessness of God. When God appeared to Moses at the burning bush in the wilderness, he introduced himself as "I AM"—an admittedly unconventional name. "I AM" is an expression of God's eternal, timeless nature: "I neither was nor will be, I AM." Ever. Fully. Present. What would it look like—if it's at all possible—to reflect the timelessness of God?

Consider how our lives are manipulated by time: the intensity of our walking pace, the weight of our foot upon the car's accelerator, even the beating of our heart. We are usually moving from somewhere to somewhere else—with something else we must do—with little patience for where we are. Because we are always on the move, most everything and everyone we encounter impedes our progress, our outcomes, our personal and professional agendas.

As a result, we become impatient: impatient with ourselves; impatient with neighbor; impatient with God. Patience, I have found, is much more than a common courtesy or virtue. Patience, like the baseball park, is a rare space of sanctuary—a space we create—that offers us a respite from the insatiable demands of time. A space where we can be fully present with ourselves, our God, our neighbor—without the sense that we should be somewhere—doing something—else. A space where everything and everyone are no longer mere impositions.

How then can we create a space of patience? Consider…First, where's the reflection or—even better—the refuge of timelessness for you? Is there a small, physical structure that you can keep at hand to remind you of this distinctive reflection or refuge? § Second, have you ever been around another who is patient, at peace, and fully engaged in the moment? What's that like? How does that person show up? How might your life change if you show up in the same way? § Third, how easily do you surrender yourself to the tyranny of the urgent? How attached are you to your progress, your outcomes, your personal and professional agendas? How does this attachment impact your attitude and your relationships? Where is it possible to loosen your grip? Fourth, remember that patience is among the fruit of the Spirit (Galatians 5:22–25). Hmm... what, then, would *impatience* suggest of our relationship with the Spirit?

Baseballer Ted Williams and golfer Sam Snead—legends in their sports and heralded as masters of their swings—used to kid each other about whose job was the more difficult. Williams often declared, "Hitting a baseball is the single most difficult thing to do in sport." In an article in *Golf Digest*, Williams recalled telling Snead that the golf ball is "just sitting there all pretty, snow white, smiling, teed up, everybody's quiet like a church." By contrast, he explained, baseball hitters face fastballs and curves from all angles with fans screaming. "Yeah, I know," said Snead, "but when we hit a foul ball, we got to go out and play it."

In 2003, Gary Mihoces of *USA Today* led an investigation to determine the "10 Hardest Things to Do in Sports." The study concluded that the ten most difficult things to do in sports, counting down to the most difficult, included skiing downhill at eighty to ninety miles per hour, stopping a soccer penalty kick, riding in the Tour de France, running a marathon, landing a quad in figure skating, returning a 130-mph tennis serve, hitting a golf ball long and straight, pole vaulting at heights in excess of fifteen feet, driving a race car at megaspeeds around a track without injury, and—with a nod to Ted Williams—hitting a baseball thrown at ninety miles per hour and beyond.

In *The Physics of Baseball*—a title that proves there's a publisher for nearly any book—retired Yale University professor Robert Adair observes that a fastball thrown at 95 to 100 mph reaches home plate in about four-tenths of one second. Four-tenths of one second. Since the batter takes about two-tenths of a second to swing the bat, he must commit to the swing when the ball is about halfway to the plate—having observed the sphere for about the same time it takes a man to voluntarily blink his eyes, the same time it takes a car's airbag to inflate. Midway through his swing, when the ball is about fifteen feet from the plate, the batter has little chance to adjust his aim. Which explains the difficulty of hitting a curve ball, since about half of a breaking pitch's deviation occurs in the final fifteen feet.

Patience, please; I'll get to the point in a moment.

Consequently, Major League batters—rather than react impulsively to the pitched ball—must instead largely mentally anticipate the trajectory, velocity, and placement of the pitch to successfully hit the baseball; while the pitcher, of course, attempts to confuse the batter's expectations. Little wonder, then, that a .300 hitter is paid millions of dollars though he will fail at the plate seven out of ten attempts.

So, what's the point?

BASEBALL AND OUR PILGRIMAGE HOME

Just this. Life, like batting a baseball, demands anticipation, intention, focus. Scripture describes this quality as moral excellence in 2 Peter 1:5. The ignoble will always win the battle of the impulse. May your purpose—your resolve—be secure.

And don't swing at bad pitches.

How might you describe the difference between reactive and proactive? § How would you describe yourself? § How essential to a proactive life is a vision that transcends the mundane? § How would you describe your vision?

Long ago, in Europe and Russia, there was a "Two-field" system of farming. Oats were generally sown in the outlying acreage. These fields were fertilized largely by turning out the cattle at night. The interior acreage—the best land, carefully tilled, manured, and sown with grains—lay nearest the house, or home. The two fields were called the infield and the outfield. The Two-field system has given way to more efficient methods of farming, but its legacy lives on in baseball.

I'm curious, what multigenerational legacies show up in you and your extended family? § What is your attachment to these legacies? Do you turn a blind eye to them? Are you largely unaware of them? Do you honor them? § Perhaps barely audible above the noise in your world today, what might your legacies be calling you to?

SAFE AT HOME!

With the final out of the World Series, stadiums are shuttered, players disperse, crowds go home. Season's end feels a bit like death; but, like life itself, there is hope for spring when life will begin anew. Until then, a brief eulogy in honor of another passing season...

Baseball Testifies to Immortality. One, there is no clock in baseball. A game of nine can be played in an hour-and-a-half, or—if the Yankees and the Red Sox are sharing the field—it might take five hours or longer. Baseball is timeless. ⁋ Two, there are no ties in baseball. In theory, a baseball game may never end. ⁋ Three, the left and right field foul lines strike out, so to speak, from home plate past third and first bases, respectfully, through the outfield, where they climb the foul poles and ascend into the endless heavens. ⁋ Four, contrary to the precise engineering of the infield, there are no prescribed boundaries to the outfield. The game could, conceivably, be played on a field without limits. ⁋ And, five, even the ball testifies to immortality. It's formed by stitching together two pieces of leather, both punched in the shape of infinity's mark.

And yet, unique to baseball among all major team sports, the player who departs the game, cannot return. And so...

Baseball testifies to mortality. So play. Play well. In this very moment.

BASEBALL AND OUR PILGRIMAGE HOME

It's easy to feel overwhelmed by the expanse and the epochs of our world and its complex, tumultuous, story. It's difficult to feel grounded by, to be connected to, something so vast and beyond our ken.

The one thread of continuity to offer clarity and stability to the story of our world is *HisStory*—the Divine Narrative of God's relentless pursuit of reconciliation with all things under heaven and earth. But, even so, the characters, communities, and cultures central to the Divine Narrative are but vague shadows on the horizon of ancient history.

And here is where baseball inserted itself into my life when I was yet a boy. I gradually came to perceive baseball as a metaphor, even a microcosm, for the Divine Narrative—compressed into little more than a century, much of which I have been fortunate enough to have witnessed.

There are a number of similarities between the Divine Narrative of scripture and the story of Major League Baseball. Consider just a few...

Like the Divine Narrative, the story of professional baseball began in Paradise. Seriously. The first organized game—played under Alexander Cartwright's rules—featured the New York Base Ball Club and the New York Knickerbockers. They played on September 23rd, 1845 in Hoboken, New Jersey's Elysian (or Greek, *Elysium*; Paradise) Fields.

Like the Divine Narrative's inception in Genesis, there is controversy around the time and place of baseball's beginning. About the only things certain today, are that baseball was not invented by Abner Doubleday; it was not first played in Cooperstown, New York; and the words, "Play ball," were not first cried out in 1839, as originally attested.

Like the Divine Narrative, however, baseball is a story of leaving home and coming home—a story of reconciliation of those who left with those who remained behind. Baseball is a story of tribe and brotherhood, of sacrifice and redemption. A story, unlike any other team sport, that can be reconstructed play by play by interpreting a game's scorecard.

Like the Divine Narrative, baseball transcends time and space. It is played without a clock, on a field that stretches forward and upward without boundaries, with a ball that is made of two pieces of leather cut in the shape of infinity, eternity.

A few other curious parallels…The Divine Narrative has houses of worship that beckon sojourning pilgrims, as baseball has stadiums that draw the faithful…The Divine Narrative's Ark of the Covenant housed its priceless treasures, as baseball's Hall of Fame in Cooperstown, New York stores the artifacts of baseball… and, as the Divine Narrative's Ethiopian cabinet official and Roman centurion Cornelius integrated the Divine Narrative, so did Jackie Robinson integrate baseball.

• • •

I only discovered the full measure of baseball as a microcosm of the Divine Narrative in May of 2000 on my first visit to Cooperstown. Until then, Babe Ruth and other historic figures of baseball existed, for me, only in faded sepia-tone photographs and other-worldly, grainy, black and white newsreels. Ruth and his fellows seemed no more accessible than—and indeed as distant as—Moses and Elijah.

But when Kathy and I walked into the museum at Cooperstown, among the first things we saw, in color and form, was a New York Yankees uniform—a broad number three sewn across its back—once worn by Babe Ruth. Here was evidence of the reality that had once cast the mere shadow I had previously known.

Proof of life.

• • •

For the first time I imagined Ruth—in the company of his teammates and opponents—spring from page to life, from shadow to reality. It was as if I had traveled back through time and space and witnessed his heroic feats for myself.

And then it struck me, if I could awaken to the legends of baseball—to see them as people, rather than mere images, participating in a nine-inning drama of home and reconciliation—what of those legends from the larger, much more ambitious story of home and reconciliation, the Divine Narrative?

Yes, I could now imagine Moses and Elijah, Jesus and Paul, and my other biblical heroes—just like Ruth and his fellows—spring from page to life, from shadow to reality. And since then, as strange as it might sound, this lovely pastoral game has deepened my ability to recognize and to step into the reality of the Divine Narrative of scripture: God's relentless pursuit of reconciliation of all things under heaven and earth.

And they say it's just a game.

SAFE AT HOME!

>Old photos

>Black and white

>Old movies

>Black and white

>Old newsreels

>Black and white

>As a child

>These flickering images of gray

>—conspicuous in a

>>world of living color—

>Seemed of a time

>>and a place far away,

>>else...

BASEBALL AND OUR PILGRIMAGE HOME

Was our world

Once without hue?

The stories of long ago,

Void of color, simply untrue?

If the Babe

Lived only in pictures

[this child once wondered]

What then of ancient stories

I trusted from scripture?

To the Hall

Baseball's history to review

Where I gratefully discovered

Ruth's pinstripes were blue

SAFE AT HOME!

THE SECOND:
THE SOUL OF THE GAME

It breaks your heart. It is designed to break your heart.

The game begins in spring, when everything else begins again,

and it blossoms in the summer, filling the afternoons and evenings,

and then as soon as the chill rains come,

it stops and leaves you to face the fall alone.

A. Bartlett Giamatti

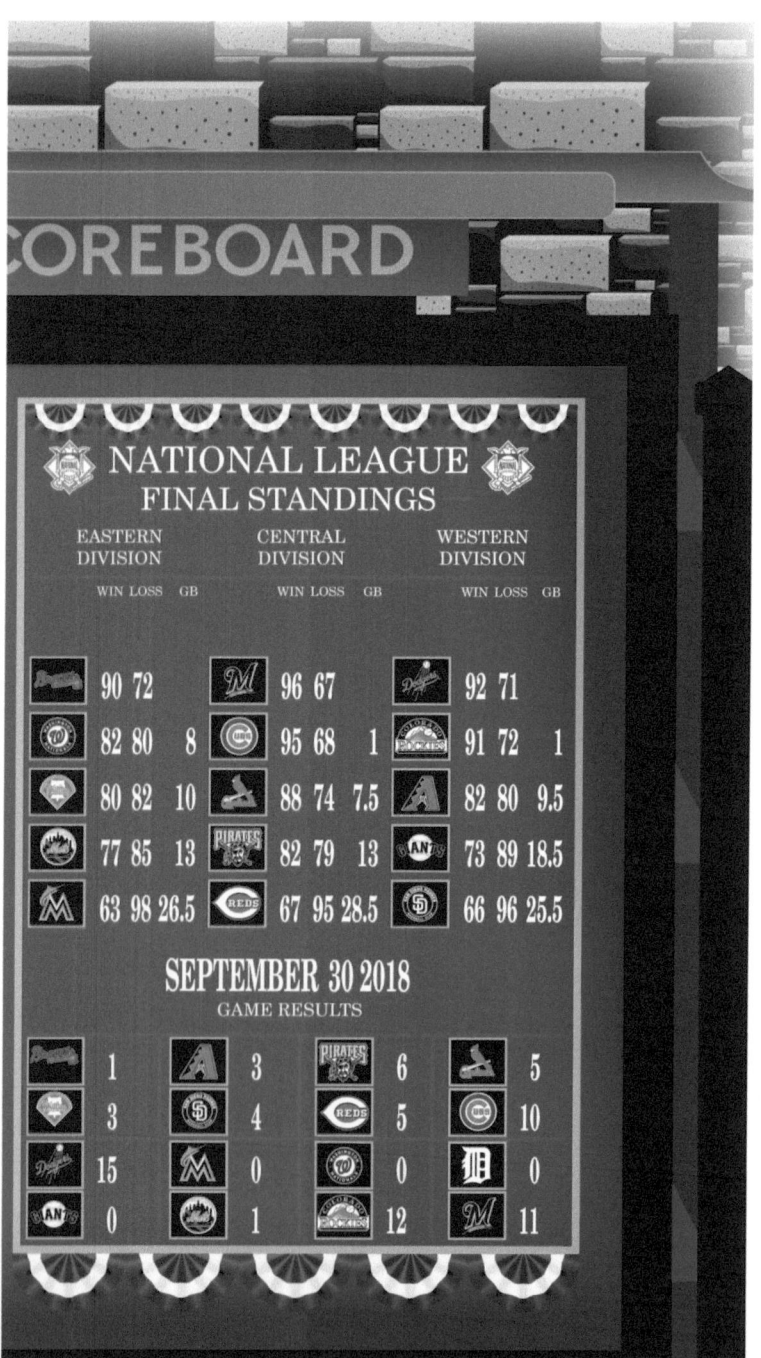

THE SECOND:
THE SOUL OF THE GAME

In the modern era of Major League Baseball—dating back to 1901—twenty perfect games have been thrown by pitchers. A perfect game in baseball is one in which a pitcher gets three up and three down in each of nine innings: no hits, no walks, no errors. Twenty perfect games out of nearly a quarter million games played.

The twenty-first perfect game in history—the third of the 2010 season alone—was tossed at Detroit's Coamerica Park, on Wednesday, June 2nd.

Well, almost... you see, the twenty-first perfect game in history was lost, well, to human imperfection.

Tigers' pitcher Armando Galarraga retired Cleveland's first twenty-six batters. With two out in the top of the ninth inning—one out shy of perfection, the hometown crowd on its feet in anticipation of history—the Indians' Jason Donald squibbed an infield ground ball to Tigers' first baseman Miguel Cabrera. Cabrera fielded the ball and tossed it to Galaragga who was covering first base. Replays—inadmissible evidence in the Court of Baseball—bear witness that Galaragga and the baseball beat Jason Donald to first base. Inexplicably, however, first base umpire Jim Joyce ruled the runner safe. Galarraga's immediate reaction to the injustice: a tilt of the head, a casual smile, and nary a word of protest. Remarkable.

The game ended with a whimper one batter later when Galaragga retired Trevor Crowe for the final out.

Perfection is oh so overrated.

Perfection is, in reality, as much a result of serendipity as of skill; perfection is, perhaps above all, noteworthy for its scarcity. Of greater value, it can be argued, is one's reconciliation to imperfection, to frailty, to disappointment. Which brings us back to umpire Jim Joyce and pitcher Armando Galarraga...

Joyce, a veteran of twenty-five seasons, reviewed the call in the umpires' room and was crestfallen when he discovered his error. "I cost that kid a perfect game," he later confessed. Still in his umpire gear, he met with Galarraga and tearfully apologized. He invited the press to his dressing room and acknowledged his mistake.

The next afternoon, the Tigers and Indians met for the closing game of the series. The umpiring rotation put Joyce behind the plate

BASEBALL AND OUR PILGRIMAGE HOME

for Thursday's game. Major League Baseball gave Joyce—the object of catcalls and, worse, threats against him and his family—the option of pulling out of the day's assignment. Joyce, however, declined the offer, stepped from the tunnel and on to the field in preparation for the game—uncertain of what awaited him.

Meanwhile, Jim Leyland—manager of the Detroit Tigers and an "old school" baseball man—had his entire team stand in front of the dugout and applaud Joyce and his fellow umpires as they stepped from the tunnel. How cool is that? The crowd took Leyland's cue and politely applauded the men in blue. Then Leyland made an unusual move and sent a player in his stead to home plate to deliver the line-up card to Jim Joyce. He sent Armando Galarraga. There at home, a visibly moved Jim Joyce and Armando Galarraga shook hands and reconciled for all to see.

In baseball, as in The Divine Narrative of scripture, nobody's perfect. Well, almost nobody. Baseball, as I have written previously, is an unfolding and unanticipated, sometimes indeed chaotic, drama of redemption—of reconciliation—a Homeresque story of coming home to the embrace of family. Armando Galarraga, Jim Joyce, Jim Leyland, and a supporting cast demonstrated that some things are better than perfection. And that, my friend, is almost...

Perfect.

Where are you driven by perfection? § How does it show up? § What's the cost? § Where's the need for reconciliation? § What's the lie? § Where lies the blessing?

SAFE AT HOME!

The highlight of my boyhood summers was spending a week or more with the Mackey boys, a family friendship that began when our mothers were teens and has endured for three generations. I lived in Lynwood, a quiet suburb of Los Angeles; the Mackeys lived across the basin in the more metropolitan city of Burbank. We rode bicycles; we collected baseball cards; we played ball. We played baseball in the park; Wiffle ball in the street; and football, well, in the Valhalla Cemetery of North Hollywood, the next town over.

Our pick-up games would inevitably attract other youngsters, most of whom took our games a lot more seriously than we did. Play devolved into aggression; smiles morphed into scowls. Mike and Mark would usually tire of the competition and exit the game first. I would follow a short time later. David would stick it out to the end.

Although I love sports as a participant and as a spectator, I find competition wearisome. Especially when it shows up in me.

All of which reminds me, curiously enough, of the Apostle Paul's contrast of the deeds (plural) of the flesh and the fruit (singular) of the Spirit (Galatians 5:19–23). The deeds of the flesh and the fruit of the Spirit comprise something of a divine assessment tool for gauging spiritual formation. Even a cursory reading suggests that most all of the qualities—from both lists—are relational. It's evidence—alongside the two foremost commands, "Love God... love neighbor"—that confirms following Jesus is all about relationship. But what do the deeds and fruit have to do with a competitive instinct?

Just this, the fruit of the Spirit reflect a sense of community; the deeds of the flesh reflect a sense of competition. A competitive nature does not inevitably lead to Paul's deeds of the flesh; it can, however, move a person from an other-oriented life to a self-oriented life.

How badly do you hate to lose? At anything. § Do your relationships and social interactions reflect a spirit of competition—the deeds of the flesh? Or do they reflect a spirit of community—the fruit of the Spirit? The quality of our relationships—with our intimates, friends, and acquaintances—tend to manifest whether we are directed by the desires of the flesh or by the desires of the Spirit. § Does your competitive spirit hinder your spiritual formation? § What's the place awaiting transformation?

In February of 1968, as a turbulent decade drew to a close, Paul Simon and Art Garfunkel withdrew to Columbia Record's New York studio and recorded one of their most enduring songs.

Mrs. Robinson became an anthem of an American generation who mourned the loss of their innocence and the passing of their heroes. The song's most memorable lyric longs for the days when baseball legend Joe DiMaggio, "The Yankee Clipper," was dependably anchored in centerfield:

SAFE AT HOME!

Where have you gone, Joe DiMaggio?
A nation turns its lonely eyes to you.
What's that you say, Mrs. Robinson,
"Joltin' Joe has left and gone away."

The familiar, mournful refrain touches a place deep within my spirit. I concede that I have less attachment to the modern iteration of Major League Baseball; my passion is for the game itself and its storied history. Gone are the heroes, the DiMaggios, their mythical exploits preserved in the flickering, grainy images of newsreels; replaced by celebrities, their feats and flaws the grist of round-the-clock media coverage. Rare is the ethic of character; replaced by the cult of personality.

And yet, from time to time—in baseball as in life—the spirit of the Yankee Clipper emerges from the shadows and we witness qualities of the heroic: self-sacrifice and endurance; grace and pluck.

How would you describe the difference between heroes and celebrities? § Who are the Joe DiMaggios in your life, then and now?. § Recall a time in your life when you responded heroically. § Who would you need to be, what would you need to do, to routinely call forth the heroic in yourself—rather than depend on the call of circumstance?

BASEBALL AND OUR PILGRIMAGE HOME

For years, prior to our move to Louisiana, we spent the week between Christmas and New Year's Day on California's Central Coast. The winter months bring mild temperatures, light winds, and fresh crab to the coast. California's Central Coast, however, is a now a bit distant for a few days of rest. From our door in Farmerville, Louisiana, it's 1,958.88 miles to the San Simeon Pines Resort in Cambria; a slightly better option is the Kon Tiki Inn on Pismo Beach, but—at 1,899.65 miles—it still seems hardly doable.

So this year we turned our sights, and our tires, to Hot Springs, Arkansas. Hot Springs is nestled within the Ouachita Mountains just a few hours up the Ouachita River from our home. The city—incorporated in 1851 but popularized for its mineral spas in the early twentieth century—is built atop numerous, well, hot springs. It's an old, and in any sense an antiquated, city; though it's redeemed by its natural beauty, its depression-era art deco structures, and the hospitality of its residents.

And, naturally, there's a baseball connection.

• • •

More than a century ago, when Major League Baseball was confined to the colder climes east and north of St. Louis, teams first sent their players south for Spring Training. But before Florida—and long before Arizona—baseball pioneers assembled in Hot Springs for physical conditioning and, perhaps chiefly, to dry out.

Babe Ruth was among those early players who enjoyed the environs of the Valley of the Vapors. In fact, it was at Whittington Park in

Hot Springs that the Babe, with one Ruthian swing of the bat, convinced management to move his considerable gifts from the pitching rotation to become a daily position player.

On St. Patrick's Day, 1918, Ruth—yet a pitcher with the Red Sox, but starting at first base against the Brooklyn Dodgers (then known as the "Robins")—hit his second home run of the game. The ball cleared the right field fence and landed across the street in the Arkansas Alligator Farm. Even the Robins stood up and cheered. It's estimated that the ball traveled 573 feet.

Baseball historian Bill Jenkinson recalls that day of Ruth's debut in the field and his two massive home runs as "the day that changed baseball forever."

• • •

I was taking a mineral bath at the historic Buckstaff Bathhouse, circa 1912, reclined in a massive tub old enough and big enough to accommodate Babe Ruth's considerable girth. And mine. I was relatively alone in the massive room of weary concrete, marble, and brass. It appeared that nothing had changed but the light bulbs since Ruth.

The mineral waters, flowing from the earth at 147,° relaxed and refreshed my body and soul; the attendant was a kindly man, an angel of sorts, an employee of nearly forty years. And all this, a full ninety minutes, for less than the cost of a California haircut.

I had the oddest sense while immersed in the churning, healing waters of the bathhouse. Surrounded by the old world elegance of another era, the aged but timeless facility felt like an ante room where one might be led after death in preparation for a better world; where the attendants welcome the weary, rinse away their impurities, refresh their spirit. It was, of course, an imaginative thought. But the thought itself remains transformative, restorative. A metaphor, perhaps, of the hope of a new world, a better world.

It was as fine as a trip to the coast.

Okay, use your imagination to give life to the details of this brief anecdote from the annals of the National Pastime.

It's October 10th, 19twenty6, Game 7 of the World Series at Yankee Stadium. For the uninitiated, the Series—a best of seven affair—is tied at three games each; therefore, the winner of this afternoon's contest will be crowned Champion.

The Yankees are trailing the Cardinals, 3 to 2, with two outs in the bottom of the ninth inning. Future Hall of Famer Grover Cleveland, "Old Pete" Alexander has fallen off the wagon and on to the mound—for St. Louis. The Yankees' hopes quicken when, down to their last out, their batsman draws a walk to put the tying runner on base. Incredibly, however, the base runner—sensing Alexander's alcohol-induced stupor—takes off on a valiant, but high-risk, gambit to steal second base and maneuver himself into scoring position. Cardinals catcher Bob O'Farrell fires the ball to second baseman Rogers Hornsby who tags the runner out on a close play.

And just like that, the 1926 World Series is over.

There's no final pitch, no final swing and miss, no final fly to deep centerfield. It's the only time in the history of the World Series that the final out was recorded on a runner caught stealing.

The lesson learned is that not even Babe Ruth—the runner caught stealing to end the '26 Series—can always be, well, Ruthian.

Ah, there's always next year, so they say.

Was it merely coincidence that, as humiliating as was the end of the 1926 season for Ruth and the Yankees, so was the 1927 edition triumphant? The 1927 Champion Yankees—whose starting line-up is to this day remembered as "Murderer's Row" and six of whom are enshrined in Cooperstown—is regarded as one of the greatest baseball teams in history. And Babe Ruth, the goat of the previous year's Game 7, enjoyed the greatest year of his legendary career. Did '27 happen because '26 happened? § What better things might come this new year from adversity endured this past year? § How do we allow our entire characters and lives to be defined by episodic setbacks: the unfortunate ending of a season, a job, a relationship, what else? § Who are you—who are your critics—not to recognize that what appears to be an unfortunate end may actually be either a cautionary speed bump or even the beginning of something better?

Ah, thank God, this is next year, so I joyfully declare!

BASEBALL AND OUR PILGRIMAGE HOME

It was a Thursday night, September 9th, 1965, when Chicago Cubs southpaw Bob Hendley, a native of Macon, Georgia, took the mound at Dodger Stadium in Los Angeles. Attendance was light; nearly half of the fifty thousand plus seats at Dodger Stadium were empty.

• • •

In the bottom half of the first inning, Hendley fielded a bunt and threw out Maury Wills for the first out. He got Jim Gilliam to fly to centerfield for the second out. And he retired the side when Willie Davis popped up to third baseman Ron Santo.

For four innings, Hendley was perfect. Each inning three Dodgers confidently stepped to the plate, and three Dodgers humbly returned to the dugout. At the halfway mark, Hendley had thrown only thirty pitches. Thirty pitches. Remarkable.

Hendley's bid for perfection, however, was frustrated in the bottom of the fifth. Dodger left fielder "Sweet" Lou Johnson drew a lead off walk. Right fielder Ron Fairly laid down a sacrifice bunt, moving Johnson to second. And on Hendley's first pitch to the next batter, second baseman Jim Lefebvre, Johnson broke for third. He safely pulled into the bag with a stolen base; and on Cubs catcher Chris Krug's wild throw to third, Johnson sprinted home with an unearned run (baseball-speak meaning the run wasn't the pitcher's responsibility).

Hendley had lost his perfect game. He now trailed 1–0 but after six innings he still had a no-hitter against the powerful Dodgers. But Lou Johnson—who had robbed Hendley of both his perfect game and his shutout in the fifth—doubled deep to first base in the bottom of the seventh to put an end to the no-hitter. (Yes, you read that right, an infield double!)

Johnson proved to be the Dodgers' only base runner in the game; his walk and double were the only blotches on Hendley's performance that lovely summer evening in Los Angeles over half a century ago. Unfortunately for Hendley and his teammates from The Windy City, the Dodgers needed only the one run to win.

• • •

For on the mound that night for the Los Angeles Dodgers, legendary hurler Sandy Koufax threw only the sixth perfect game in the modern era of Major League Baseball.

It was a bummer of a night to throw a one-hitter.

It just goes to show you, don't ever measure your worth or your work against another.

> Not that we dare to classify or compare ourselves with some of those who are commending themselves. But when they measure themselves by one another and compare themselves with one another, they are without understanding (The Apostle Paul, 2 Corinthians 10:12).

BASEBALL AND OUR PILGRIMAGE HOME

An evening at the ballpark these days is a full-sensory experience. There's the press of the crowd, shoulder to shoulder—their alternating, celebratory shouts and taunting jeers; the loud horns and music; the fragrant smoke of hot dogs and ribs, poultry and more; the partisan catcalls—and worse—among fans of both teams.

And that's just in the parking lot.

Ballparks have evolved over the century of modern baseball, from wooden—and thus flammable—band boxes to concrete and steel, tiered jewel boxes to multi-purpose domed boxes, to state-of-the art, faux vintage parks filled with all of the modern amenities including luxury boxes.

But, every morning of the baseball season, when all of the stadiums' seats and corridors have been emptied, the lights and noise have been dialed down, and the pitchers' mounds have been covered with tarp, something lovely happens in the charming village of Cooperstown, New York. A member of the staff emerges from the alcove of the National Baseball Hall of Fame. He carries a box of numbers to the modest, old-school scoreboard in front of the museum. There, he manually posts, one number at a time, the scores, and he updates the standings based upon the previous night of games in the far-off stadiums of North America.

It's an unofficial ritual and a reminder that baseball—regardless of its cosmetic changes, its player-turned-celebrity culture, its grand but costly venues—remains grounded in the pastoral game of another era. Baseball, though it may not reflect the testosterone-infused battles of football and basketball, has remained the National Pastime for a reason.

It has welcomed, though oft begrudgingly, elements of contemporary culture, but its roots remain grounded in the rich soils of a weathered past.

Baseball's fans are passionate about their game. Some, regardless of their age, believe the rules of the game to be sacrosanct—never to be altered. They prefer pitchers to bat for themselves and designated hitters to shop for a glove. Fans on the other side of the aisle believe the rules of the game need to be altered to encourage a younger, restless, more savvy audience. They believe the game is too long, too slow, too old.

And, of course, we see similar polarization across political, religious, and cultural divides. May we—whether young or old—never be so arrogant to think that we alone have clarity of vision. May we never accept that multiplication comes through division. May we respect the integrity of the endeavor without sacrificing instinct and compassion. May we be grounded in the perennial truths of proven wisdom, while delighting in discoveries that nurture life, light, and love. May we remember that we all—with a mix of courage and concern—are trying to find our way home.

And may we recall and emulate the quiet and faithful fellow in Cooperstown who, when the lights and noise have faded, knows the score.

BASEBALL AND OUR PILGRIMAGE HOME

The old photo is heartbreaking. It's February 23rd, 1960. Some two hundred Dodgers fans are scattered among the thousands of empty seats in Brooklyn's Ebbets Field. They're joined by a group of former players including Otto Miller, catcher in the inaugural game played at Ebbets in 1913, and Roy Campanella, catcher in the final game played at Ebbets in 1957. A crane has encroached upon the sanctity of the field; the crane's at work, where men once played. A wrecking ball, sardonically painted as a baseball, has plummeted from the crane's tower and has crushed the visitors' dugout.

Low and inside. Strike.

Although I grew up in the shadow of Dodgers Stadium in Los Angeles, I have a deep and abiding affinity for the Brooklyn Dodgers, the team affectionately known, locally, as "Dem Bums" and later, universally in their final decade, as "The Boys of Summer." It was an era when the Dodgers starting second baseman might have been your next door neighbor, and likely would have "walked to work" every afternoon—just another "Trolley Dodger" (as pedestrians were known a century ago in Brooklyn)—alongside fans attending the game at Ebbets Field.

I've only been to Brooklyn once and then only briefly, to change trains at an eerie subterranean station. I was born two years after Dodgers owner Walter O'Malley moved the Dodgers West in '57, born the very year the Los Angeles iteration of the team won its first World Series in '59. Our home, however—for reasons that are deeply held, yet difficult to articulate—retains far more artifacts from Brooklyn than from Los

Angeles. Scores of baseball cards of the era; signatures from many heroes of the franchise including Snyder, Koufax, Drysdale, Roe, Newcombe, Branca, Alston, Scully, and others; scorecards and yearbooks; postcards of Ebbets Field and even a brick rescued from the rubble of its demolition.

It's difficult to imagine the neighborhood's pain—grieving the loss of identity, community, and hope—when for three years the old stadium sat empty, silent, and dark—while the rest of the world played baseball.

• • •

The photograph of mourners gathered in the stands of Ebbets Field resonates with me tonight. I'm on my way to California. A week ago, my elderly parents' lives were unhurried and routine. Today, my mother is under the care of hospice. Cancer.

Low and inside. Strike.

Though her body is sick, her spirit prospers. The woman who taught me how to live, will doubtless teach me how to die. It's difficult, however, to imagine the imminent loss of the woman who has defined the calling and the spirit of our family.

It's a reminder—neither good nor bad, just a reminder—that life is best lived with lovingkindness and a gentle grip.

• • •

Time passes. Today the Dodgers have played more games in beautiful Dodger Stadium, sitting above the fray in Los Angeles, than they played in Ebbets Field. Most of Brooklyn has gotten past the move; the rest are still alive. Only a handful from the Brooklyn ball club remain in the Dodgers' employ: most notably, Hall of Fame broadcaster and voice of my childhood, Vin Scully.

In 1991, Scully—today, a sixty-odd year veteran of the booth—was calling a game pitting the Dodgers against Chicago's Cubs. During the broadcast, Scully reported on injured superstar Andre Dawson. "Andre Dawson," Scully melodically reported, "has a bruised knee and is listed as day to day."

After a few moments of reflection, Scully rhetorically asked, "Aren't we all?"

Indeed. Live with lovingkindness and a gentle grip.

No questions. It's enough to just sit quietly with the learning.

SAFE AT HOME!

THE THIRD:
TIME AND SPACE

A baseball game that is tied at the end of nine innings

continues, without end, into extra innings until the winning run is scored;

a baseball game in theory, may be played without resolution, without end.

Critics of the game contend a game of baseball is slow,

when in fact it is neither slow nor fast. It just is.

Michael Fox

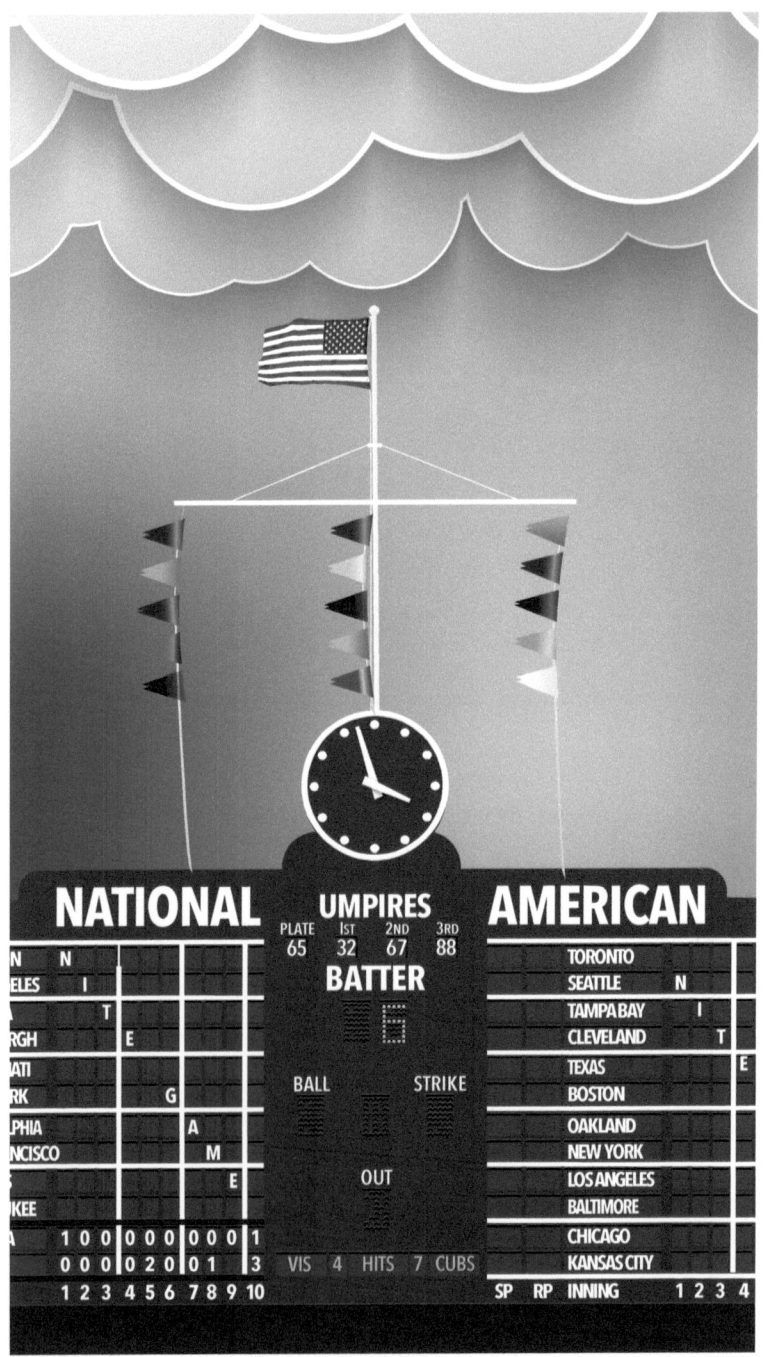

THE THIRD:

TIME AND SPACE

Baseball—as readers may have gathered by now—has been a compass rose on my pilgrimages near and far, a trusted third base coach beckoning me home, and, indeed, baseball represents home itself—its fields and cathedrals proxies for a homeplace relinquished long ago.

In September 2008, I met my nephews—Daniel and Kevin, and Kevin's son Andrew Michael—in New York City for two games during the final week of the baseball season and, lamentably, the final week in the life of The Yankee Stadium, circa 1923. It would be Daniel and Kevin's first trip to "The House that Ruth Built," and Andrew's first experience of a Major League Baseball game. The pilgrimage to The Yankees Stadium was a wondrous sequel to a summer day some twenty-five years prior when I carried young Daniel and Kevin to their first ballgame—

then on the opposite coast—to witness New York's Mets play the home team at Dodger Stadium.

Our day (and, incidentally, Andrew's third birthday) began in Midtown Manhattan. We spent the morning exploring the city—walking north in the general direction of the Bronx; then, following lunch in the crowded basement of the Carnegie Deli, we took Andrew to work off some energy on the playground at the southern end of Central Park. Afterward, we found a secluded stand of trees on a gently sloping knoll of the park. There we rested neath the passing clouds of the autumn sky on a serene oasis in the midst of one of the busiest cities in the world.

It's difficult to recall just how long we napped in Central Park before we boarded the jarring subway ride to East 161st Street. It was one of those rare moments when, in contrast to the world around us, time stood still. It's difficult to describe in English the sense of such moments; the Greeks' expansive vocabulary, however, has two words for time that are helpful in understanding a time-outside-of-time moment: chronos and kairos.

Chronos time is chronological time, clock time. Sophisticated clocks, in fact, are sometimes referred to as "chronometers." Chronos time is, as one has described: "The passing of spring, summer, fall, winter. Or morning, noon, and night. It has a beginning, middle, and an end." Chronos time is a taskmaster; by it we measure our lives.

Kairos time, by contrast, is an opportune or appointed time. Jesus used the word kairos when he declared, "The time (kairos) is fulfilled, and the kingdom of God is at hand" (Mark 1:15). Kairos is a moment of undetermined time in which something special, something transcendent, occurs.

Kairos time indeed transcends chronos time. Chronos is measured in minutes; kairos is measured in moments. We *do* in chronos; we are allowed to *be* in kairos. Chronos is valued in quantitative terms; kairos is valued in qualitative terms. Chronos is about speed; kairos is about space. We may live in chronos, but we long for kairos.

That day in Central Park, in the heart of New York's metropolis, chronos time throbbed all about us, evidenced by clouds passing, shadows falling, horns honking, people scurrying. But there on that shaded knoll—as again later in the evening at the ballpark—my beloved nephews and I were immersed in kairos time: a-time-outside-of-time moment.

What comes up for you when you think of kairos time? § When you cry out, "I need more time!," are you craving chronos time or kairos time? § What might it take for you to carve out kairos space in your chronos schedule?

I noticed, over time, that only one of the two elevators in the hotel lobby functioned. The set of doors on the right would respond to the push of the button; the set of doors on the left remained curiously shut and still.

Of course, it's likely that the hotel—a posh but aged beauty—had shut down the elevator to save money. Ah—but in my imagination—there was another explanation. The set of doors on the left opened only by a mysterious key and led, not to an elevator, but to an enchanted conveyance capable of transporting its occupant across time and space.

Oh, I wish I had that key.

But where would I go? My first thought—apart from a place and time compelled by family or faith and inspired by this weekend's renewal of Major League Baseball—would be to travel back in time to 1950 and attend what at the time would have appeared to have been a meaningless spring training baseball game in Florida. There the Philadelphia Athletics took the field in Vero Beach to play the host Brooklyn Dodgers, two teams that would eventually call California home.

In the Athletics' dugout was a slender, weary, old man wearing—as he had for half a century and nearly 8,000 games—a tailored black suit with a starched collar and tie and matching hat. His name was Connie Mack, born Cornelius McGillicuddy during the War of Northern Aggression. Mack had owned and managed the A's for fifty years. Pitcher Bobby Shantz recalled the one occasion when he saw Mr. Mack concede his formal attire during a ballgame: "It was in St. Louis. The temperature was in the high nineties and it was extremely humid. The heat must have really gotten to Mr. Mack—understandably so, as he was in his eighties by then—because he took off his hat and loosened his tie. It was the only time I ever saw him out of uniform."

BASEBALL AND OUR PILGRIMAGE HOME

In the broadcast booth that spring day in 1950, was a red-headed young man anxiously calling his first game as a Dodgers broadcaster. Vin Scully, according to my *Dodgers 1950 Yearbook*, was "a 1949 Fordham University graduate who in his closing college days covered Rams football, basketball, and baseball games over the school station after lettering for two years as an outfielder on the diamond." Upon graduation, Red Barber—legendary broadcaster and, at the time, Sports Director for CBS Radio Network—had recruited Scully to call college football games. Scully impressed his employer by calling a football game from the roof of frigid Fenway Park in Boston, despite having left his coat and gloves at the hotel. (He had assumed he'd be calling the game from the warmth of the press box.) Barber subsequently recommended Scully for the empty chair beside him in the Dodgers broadcast booth. Sixty-three years later, Scully remains as the voice of the Dodgers and—in many respects—the voice of the game itself.

Looking back on that spring day in Vero Beach when Connie Mack and Vin Scully crossed paths, their storied careers together span the entire history of modern Major League Baseball, birthed in 1903. I'm curious who might have recently crossed Vin Scully's path and will continue the conversation fifty years from now.

Incidentally, the A's first baseman for that spring training game was Ferris Fain, the uncle of Shirley George, a treasured friend in the Sacramento area of California. Ah, connections.

So, if I loaned you the key to the elevator door on the left where would you go? Choose anywhere apart from the prompt of family and faith. § What personal, compelling, passion would be served by your choice?

Okay, I will own that, from time to time, I envy God. No, it's not about the whole omnipotent, walk on water, thunderbolt and lightning ,very, very frightening thing. I can't even drive a standard transmission. Multi-tasking is not a standard feature for my model.

I envy God from the perspective of time and distance.

I envy God for his transcendence over time and distance.

Time and distance are the source of heartbreak, disappointment, delusion, frustration, and possibly the occasional outbreak of hives. We are forever either working on bridging time and distance or mourning our inability to engineer it.

Time and distance interfere with our relationships. Time and distance are the stuff that our dreams are 'fraid of. Time and distance—in cahoots with their distant cousin, Filthy Lucre—are responsible for the leaks in many bucket lists. Time and distance are the authors of the top two selling phrases in the English language: "What might have been," and, "If only I had..." Have you ever uttered the phrase, "I was just a tad short?" I'm going to make up that the word tad began life as an acronym.

Time and distance.

BASEBALL AND OUR PILGRIMAGE HOME

. . .

My resentment around time and distance—as well as these feelings of envy for God—were renewed this past week when I was reading about, you guessed it, Ty Cobb.

In the decade leading up to the Roaring Twenties—the decade when celebrity became an industry—one of the most recognizable names in the country belonged to a baseball player, Ty Cobb, of the Detroit Tigers. In 1916, to test Cobb's name recognition, a newspaper in Syracuse, New York assigned its editorial cartoonist to post an envelope with drawings of a necktie and a corncob in lieu of an address. The letter was dropped in a mailbox, and a few days later, reached Ty Cobb at his home in Augusta, Georgia.

Well, this past week, I learned that Cobb's Tigers held Spring Training in 1911, right here in Monroe, just a half hour from our home. I can visit the location where those pioneers of the National Pastime assembled to prepare for the season. Try as I might, however, I can see neither them nor any indication they were once there. I'm in the right place, at the wrong time. Yet, again. There's a frustration—as foolish as it might sound—that I cannot somehow peer into another layer of time to witness baseball's immortals doing calisthenics, taking batting practice, shagging flys. Right. There. Right. Now.

Time and distance.

. . .

Stick with me, now. I've just a tad more.

As I've grown older—older, mind you, not old—I've noticed a growing sense around longing and loss. And it too feels related to our inability to bridge time and distance. It might begin as an inexplicable feeling of dissolution and darkness. It can be accompanied by the thought that even home doesn't feel like home anymore. It might grow into a sense of being cast adrift. Cast away.

It can be tempting to surrender to these vague feelings of dis-ease—to be unaware they are shared by all men and women for whom life and death seem to be governed by the face and hands of a soulless clock. These emotions might bring us to despair; or, at best, we might resign ourselves to a maudlin sentimentality.

But the truth, I believe, is so much richer. I've come to sense the tender grace of God in the midst of these feelings of detachment. Mightn't it be that within this sense of separation—deepening and darkening with the shedding of tears and years—God is slowly and gently loosening our moorings on this side of the waters. And, he's graciously, mercifully, redirecting our longing to a shore where...

Time and distance.

Are no more.

BASEBALL AND OUR PILGRIMAGE HOME

Sometimes in the stillness of a Friday evening in rural northeastern Louisiana, I wonder. Are the crowds really gathering tonight in Chavez Ravine for a Dodgers home game? Is Lemon Grass Restaurant in Sacramento really serving lamb chops tonight, accompanied by garlic noodles and fragrant Asian vegetables? Are vacationers really walking Cambria's wooden pathways overlooking the surf as the sun withdraws beyond the western horizon?

Though I'm not there? Though it's impossible for me to see?

It's a bit like the child whose curiosity wonders aloud, "Does the refrigerator light really turn off when you shut its door?"

Of course, when I'm sitting in the dining room of Lemon Grass Restaurant a couple of times a year in Sacramento, eating lamb chops, accompanied by garlic, noodles and fragrant Asian vegetables, I wonder. Are my family and friends back home really preparing to settle into the quiet of a Friday evening in rural northeastern Louisiana?

Though I'm not there? Though it's impossible for me to see?

Sometimes, family and friends and the familiar—all of those lovely elements that add up to home—seem a world away, a reality away. But my imagination allows me to cross time and space to see what otherwise cannot be seen.

And so, it feels a lot like faith.

Faith, the writer of Hebrews explains, "is what assures us our hopes will be realized; it is what convinces us of the reality that we cannot see.

And just so, in the stillness of a Friday evening in rural northeastern Louisiana, my imagination knows, my faith is certain—just as surely as the crowds are gathering tonight in Chavez Ravine for a Dodgers home game—there is a place, a home I've not seen, a world away, a reality away. But my faith allows me to cross time and space to see what otherwise cannot be seen.

Author Tom Boswell famously wrote, *Why Time Begins on Opening Day*. We plan to be at MinuteMade Park in Houston for this year's first of 162 games that will carry me through the dog days of summer and into autumn—the season that makes the rest of the calendar jealous.

Major League Baseball teams change field managers as often as I change socks.

Now before you make assumptions about my personal hygiene, let me just add, teams change managers a lot. Over five hundred men have managed ball clubs over the course of Major League Baseball's modern era (1901 forward). Remarkably, three among those five hundred plus managers—men who held court in dugouts of the early twentieth century—have had an enduring legacy of influence upon succeeding generations.

Those three men—Connie Mack of the Pittsburgh Pirates (1894–96) and the Philadelphia As (1901–50); Miller Huggins of the St. Louis

Cardinals (1913–1917) and the New York Yankees (1918–1929); and John McGraw of the Baltimore Orioles (1899, 1901–02) and the New York Giants (1902–32)—managed for over 100 years between them. Each of them was a pioneer and an innovator; each of them developed his own unique approach to the game.

Connie Mack, the "Tall Tactician," sought players who were intelligent, mannered, and self-disciplined. So, it's no surprise Mr. Mack shunned the uniform and, instead, wore a three-piece suit in the dugout. Miller Huggins, the "Mighty Mite," was originally a proponent of small ball featuring scrappy base hits and aggressive base running; his style changed when the team acquired Babe Ruth. Go figure. John McGraw, the "Little Napoleon" or "Mugsy," knew the rules, and he bent the rules; he was, at times, ill-tempered, but nevertheless an innovator who introduced or promoted many strategies common to the contemporary game including the hit-and-run play and pitching in relief.

In 2015, ESPN's Steve Wulf researched the bloodlines of all thirty active big league managers. Now, the Jews of the first century had their influential rabbinical schools, most notably the House of Hillel and the House of Shammai. Well, it turns out that baseball similarly has the House of Mack, the House of Huggins, and the House of McGraw. Wulf's research confirmed what many in baseball had long assumed. Most modern managers—including all thirty who managed in the 2015 season—could trace their managerial family tree to at least one of three managerial schools of thought: Mack, Huggins, or McGraw.

Joe Maddon, to illustrate, skipper of—dare we say it aloud, The 2016 World Champion Chicago Cubs—coached and managed in the Angels' system under Gene Mauch, who played for Billy Southworth, who played for McGraw. Other examples among many include the Los Angeles Angels' Mike Scioscia, who played for Del Crandall, who played for Charlie Grimm, who played for Mack. The Kansas City Royals' Ned Yost played for George Bamberger, who played for Leo Durocher, who played for Miller Huggins. The former Los Angeles Dodgers' Don Mattingly played for Yogi Berra, who played for Casey Stengel, who played for John McGraw. You get the idea.

Intriguing, too, is the fact that all three of these influential managers—Mack, Huggins, and McGraw—played for Ned Hanlon, manager of, most notably, the Baltimore Orioles (1892–1898) and the Brooklyn Superbas (1899–1905), later known as the Brooklyn Trolley Dodgers. Ned Hanlon would be the Adam atop the genealogical records of modern Major League Baseball managers.

So, what's the connection, the relevance? Just this. If you were to belong to a school of thought—personally, professionally, philosophically—whose school might it be? § What distinctions might you have inherited from your ancestors? § If you were to become a school of thought to future generations, what might distinguish its students? § What qualities or abilities would you choose to distinguish its students? § Who might you be, what might you do, now, to begin living into that aspiration?

BASEBALL AND OUR PILGRIMAGE HOME

What can you learn from catchers, pitchers, and second basemen? More than you might think.

As of the summer of 2014, 312 people have been elected to the National Baseball Hall of Fame in Cooperstown, New York. Among the honorees are twenty-two managers—arguably the most respected skippers in the history of Major League Baseball.

Now, here's where it gets compelling. Of the twenty-two Hall of Fame managers, fifteen—fully two-thirds of them—played catcher, pitcher, or second base before assuming the helm of a ball club:

Walter Alston (1B); Sparky Anderson (2B); Bobby Cox (3B); Leo Durocher (SS/2B); Rube Foster (P); Ned Hanlon (CF); Bucky Harris (2B); Miller Huggins (2B); Tony La Russa (IF); Tommy Lasorda (P); Al Lopez (C); Connie Mack (C); Joe McCarthy (2B); John McGraw (3B); Bill McKechnie (IF); Wilbert Robinson (C); Frank Selee (P); Billy Southworth (OF); Casey Stengel (OF); Joe Torre (C/1B/3B); Earl Weaver (2B).

Catchers, pitchers, second basemen: players who share an imaginary line bisecting the infield—literally in the middle of the action. Catchers, pitchers, second basemen: players who, from the catbird seat, are tasked to direct the movements of their teammates on the field. Catchers, pitchers, second basemen: players who learn to lead between the lines before they are called to manage from the bench.

Similarly, scripture's Timothy—groomed to lead by the Apostle Paul—established his skills in the field before he was given a place of responsibility. Paul wrote of Timothy's "proven worth" to the first-century church at Philippi of Macedonia:

> *I hope in the Lord Jesus to send Timothy to you shortly, so that I also may be encouraged when I learn of your condition. For I have no one else of kindred spirit who will genuinely be concerned for your welfare. For they all seek after their own interests, not those of Christ Jesus. But you know of his proven worth...(Philippians 2:19–24).*

Whether in business, in ministry, or on the ball field, men and women do not assume a position of leadership in a responsible organization. Hall of Fame caliber leaders first develop and demonstrate the skill, character, and experience to lead; only then are they called to serve in positions of leadership.

What is your experience around leadership? Can you sense the difference between those who are desperate to be placed in a position of authority and those who have been groomed to lead? § Of the fifteen Hall of Fame managers listed above, only two or three might have made the Hall based upon their qualifications as a player. Why do stellar players rarely make good leaders? (You might find an idea in Paul's words to the Philippians, cited previously.) § Consider the truth of this statement: "Great leaders are not those who bring out the best in themselves; great leaders are those who bring out the best in others."

BASEBALL AND OUR PILGRIMAGE HOME

It's August 2nd, one day after Major League Baseball's annual Trade Deadline. Eighteen deals were made. Forty-nine players suddenly, in many cases without warning, changed their return address yesterday. One troubled young star wasn't told where he was going, only that he wouldn't be joining his fellows on the team's flight out of town. It can get cold under the August sun.

The Trade Deadline is the day when thirty teams must decide if they'll be watching the postseason—less than two months out—from the dugout or from their couch. Thirty teams must determine if they're buying or selling talent. Thirty teams must decide: "What lies ahead: a strong winner or a long winter?" For teams that surrender to a losing season, there remain two months of meaningless games, diminishing crowds, and uncertain futures. Some baseball insiders call it The Grind.

The Grind is not in the peak experiences of brilliance. A pitcher throws a game-ending third strike on the outside corner to fool the batter, who goes down, scarcely lifting his bat from his shoulder. Or, a batter hits a ground ball with eyes that skips through the infield to score the winning run from second base.

The Grind is not in the brief valleys of adversity. A pitcher misses several starts due to a lower back injury. A batter is benched because his sense of timing at the plate is off, and fat pitches mockingly elude the exaggerated swing of his bat.

No, The Grind is playing 162 baseball games over the course of six months. The Grind is when your home games are in Los Angeles, but your home is in West Virginia. The Grind is August 2nd, and your team has traded their best players for future prospects—opting for a time of rebuilding.

The Grind is the plateau that stretches, seeming endlessly, between the peaks and the valleys.

The plateau is monotony. The plateau is a long walk in the same direction. On the plateau, no adversary threatens pursuit. No triumph is imminent. There's no adrenaline to lubricate the wheels of courage. The plateau is where we are joined on the journey by interior voices that question our ability and worth. The plateau is the space where only internal fortitude compels endurance, completion. Scripture might describe The Grind as the wilderness.

But, the plateau—and, again, not on the mountains or in the valleys—is where the character of men and women is defined and refined. One has said, "Strength of character is the ability to carry out the resolve, long after the emotion is gone."

Of course, when you're on the plateau, you can at least be grateful you haven't been traded to Cleveland.

Under what circumstances do you most feel you are on the plateau? § What intention might you now bring to the plateau that would encourage you to endure and overcome? § How might you find joy walking the plateau? §

BASEBALL AND OUR PILGRIMAGE HOME

When I was growing up in Lynwood, California, a suburb of Los Angeles, I'd grab my mitt and ball after school and pitch a simulated baseball game with my pitchback—a taut net stretched within a frame that stood in for a catcher. The pitchback would return either ground balls, or line drives, or fly balls in my direction. I must tell you... I made the most spectacular defensive plays that have never been seen. In my imagination, however, very few batters ever got any wood on the ball. More often than not, I'd pitch the ball past the stunned, imaginary batter, and the appreciative, imaginary catcher would leisurely toss the ball back to me on my imaginary mound. What a lovely pastime for a baseball-loving loner.

I still have a pitchback in the backyard. Our Lucy, however, assumes it's somehow designed for dogs; she delights in intercepting the ball before it returns to my mitt. Consequently, the pitchback goes largely unused these days.

But I do think of the pitchback from time to time. It shows up as a metaphor whenever I hear well-meaning apprentices of Jesus speak of "surrendering his burdens to Jesus"; "laying her problems at the feet of the Lord"; or "casting their cares upon him." I've tried all of those. And maybe it's just me, but—like the pitchback—Jesus keeps throwing them back to me. Swing and a miss.

But, then, maybe my expectations, like the imaginary batters whom I stared down as a boy, are unrealistic. A cardinal rule (can I say, a Dodgers rule?) common to both counseling and coaching is, "Never try to 'fix' anyone;" never assume responsibility for changing the poor behavior of another. We can be reasonably certain we're trying to fix someone and their issues if we're working harder on them than they are. Change must come from within; change—and learning—occur from working through the process.

Why then do I assume that God will behave any differently and step in and fix me and my stuff?

On the eve of his crucifixion, Jesus had a prime opportunity to intervene in the life of the apostle Peter, to fix him: "Simon, Simon, Satan has asked to sift each of you like wheat." Jesus empathized with Peter and even feared the inevitable danger that the young, naive disciple faced. However, the best that Jesus could promise Peter was this: "I have pleaded in prayer for you, Simon, that your faith should not fail. So when you have repented and turned to me again, strengthen your brothers" (Luke 22:31–32).

Although, then, Jesus will not assume ownership of our issues, he does offer this assurance, "I will plead in prayer for you." Prayer—defined by Dallas Willard—is, "Talking to God about what we are doing together" (*The Divine Conspiracy*, p. 242).

You may have a sense of aloneness. "But I will plead in prayer for you; I will talk to God about what we are doing together." You may endure hardship. "But I will plead in prayer for you; I will talk to God about what we are doing together." You may experience loss. "But I will plead in prayer for you; I will talk to God about what we are doing together."

This assurance is the essence of the high priestly ministry of Jesus: *So then, since we have a great High Priest who has entered heaven, Jesus the Son of God, let us hold firmly to what we believe. This High Priest of ours understands our weaknesses, for he faced all of the same testings we do, yet he did not sin. So let us come boldly to the throne of our gracious God. There we will receive his mercy, and we will find grace to help us when we need it most* (Hebrews 4:14–16, NLT).

What's one issue that you keep surrendering to Jesus, and he in kind keeps surrendering back to you? § If Jesus' assurance is, "But I will plead in prayer for you; I will talk to God about what we are doing together," how might you best facilitate and join his efforts?

After two days of Los Angeles traffic jams, I'm feeling—to borrow a phrase from soul artist Larry Graham of Graham Central Station—"stomped, beat-up, and whooped."

Yesterday evening, a twenty-mile journey from our hotel to Dodger Stadium took ninety minutes. Ninety minutes. During which I was cut off and scowled at, flipped off and growled at. Many urban motorists seem to be driven by a sense of urgency, an instinct of self-preservation—perhaps believing a lone parking space remains unoccupied at journey's end, and all but the lucky one will be condemned to endlessly circle the block. In traffic. With a full bladder.

Curiously, the foremost thought in my mind—well, candidly, the next-to-the-foremost thought in my mind—was the truth spoken by Paul, Love "does not seek its own." It's not that these motorists need to learn to drive (okay, the young lady in the gray Toyota needs to learn to drive); rather, they need to learn to love. In 1 Corinthians 13, Paul wrote:

> *Love is patient, love is kind and is not jealous; love does not brag and is not arrogant, does not act rudely; it does not seek its own, is not irritable, and it keeps no record of being wronged, does not rejoice about injustice but rejoices whenever the truth wins out; bears all things, believes all things, hopes all things, endures all things. Love never fails.*

Three essential truths of this passage are often overlooked.

One, the qualities of love listed in 1 Corinthians 13 form less a prescription ("Here is what you need to do...") and more an assessment ("Is this who you are?").

Two, the love of 1 Corinthians 13 is not a love of our own creation; it is, instead, "the love of God [that] has been poured out within our hearts through the Holy Spirit who was given to us" (Romans 5:5). The qualities of love listed in 1 Corinthians 13 then reflect the depth and quality of our relationship with God.

Three, although a loving relationship with God and neighbor requires surrender, it reciprocates with freedom. How much soul-draining energy do we expend in just impatience, self-promotion, seeking our own, righting perceived injustices, and keeping record of being wronged?

So, as I make my way back to the quiet intersection of Highway 2 and Highway 828 in Louisiana, I'd encourage urban motorists to learn to love. And to use their turn signals, for crying out loud.

In 1928, a twenty-one year old man born in tiny Bastrop, Louisiana—a short drive from our home in Farmerville—stepped off the train in the Bronx and on to the field of Yankee Stadium. Yankee Stadium was just five years old when Bill Dickey donned the catcher's gear—or, as he famously christened it, "the tools of ignorance"—and took his position behind home plate. Imagine what it must have been like for this young man from early twentieth-century, rural Louisiana as he watched the New York Yankees—now, his Yankees—prepare for the afternoon game!

There, just down the first base line, was Lou Gehrig. Dickey and Gehrig would become roommates and best friends by the time Gehrig's career, and his life, came to an all too sudden end thirteen years later. In fact, if you watch the classic film Pride of the Yankees, starring Gary Cooper as Lou Gehrig, you'll see Bill Dickey playing, well, Bill Dickey. From all that I've read, he really nailed the part.

Beyond Gehrig, out on the right field grass was the Sultan of Swat himself, Babe Ruth. In addition to Ruth and Gehrig, a host of baseball immortals filled Dickey's view that afternoon; for the 1928 Yankees, the defending World Champions, had a still-to-this-day-record nine future Hall of Famers on their roster.

Including rookie catcher Bill Dickey, of Bastrop, Louisiana.

But this short reflection is less about Bill Dickey, in particular, and more about legacy. Who could have imagined, that first day on the field, that Bill Dickey would influence Yankee catchers for nearly a century?

Dickey himself played catcher, baseball's most physically demanding position, for eighteen years. He was selected for eleven All-Star Games including the first in 1933. The Yankees competed in nine World Series with Bill Dickey behind the plate; they won eight of them. Bill Dickey retired in 1946, and was summoned to Cooperstown in 1954.

Twice, the Yankees lured Dickey out of retirement to serve as a coach—and he contributed to another half-dozen Yankees World Series Championships.

He was first hired in 1949 to mentor a short but powerfully-built outfielder from St. Louis. Dickey would transform a young Yogi Berra into one of the greatest catchers in Major League Baseball history. As a youngster, under the tutelage of Dickey, Berra said, "Bill is learnin' me his experience." In later years, Yogi would acknowledge, with a tad more sophistication, "I owe everything I did in baseball to Bill Dickey."

Dickey returned in 1959–60 to mentor Berra's replacement, a

young man recruited from the Negro Leagues, Elston Howard. The Yankees were one of the last teams to integrate; but, in 1955—eight years after the Dodgers' Jackie Robinson broke the color barrier—the team added the young outfielder to their roster. As they had with Berra, the Yankees asked Bill Dickey to groom Elston Howard to become the team's everyday backstop.

Bill Dickey's career with the Yankees—as a player and later as a coach—spanned the eras from Ruth to Gehrig to DiMaggio to Mantle. But his star pupil, Yogi Berra, "paid it forward." Berra passed his predecessor's torch to yet another generation of Yankees backstops, mentoring young catchers well past his eightieth birthday.

The last Yankee catcher to benefit from the accumulated wisdom of Bill Dickey and Yogi Berra was Jorge Posada, who retired in 2011 after seventeen years in pinstripes.

Nearly a century after Bill Dickey stepped off of the train in the Bronx and on to the field of Yankee Stadium.

I visited with Autumn recently, ahead of her seasonal return, and was pleased to find that we have a great deal in common.

As it turns out, we share preference for three of the four Myers-Briggs dichotomies. I'm an INTP (Introvert, Intuition, Thinking, Perceiving); she's an INFP (Introvert, Intuition, Feeling, Perceiving).

And, truth be told, we're not too far apart on the whole Thinking/Feeling function.

We're both partial to November. We delight to see the turning of the leaves. We love the crisp, cold mornings of the season. We're quite sentimental, and we enjoy time with cherished family and friends around the hearth. We long for the season's stillness to read and to reflect and to write. We both look forward to the return of the constellation Orion in the night sky. And, get this, it turns out she's a huge baseball fan; she hosts the World Series every year—something she prefers to call, "The Fall Classic." Now, you might think she's being a bit presumptuous about that one, but I too must admit some pride, knowing Fox Sports holds the television rights to the Series.

In spite of our commonalities, during our visit I confessed my profound disappointment in her. A sense of betrayal, even.

You see, over the past three years, I've suffered significant leavings while in the company of Autumn. The first—less a loss but, nevertheless, a difficult transition—was the move from our beloved hometown of twenty years, Auburn, California. The following year, we suffered the loss of Gracie, one of two canine littermates we've loved for a quarter of our lives. Last year, it was the stunning, albeit merciful, passing of my mother. And this year, on the cusp of Autumn, there was the inexplicable loss of my youngest brother, Mark.

Autumn and I talked for some time. She explained that, among the ancients, suffering didn't have the sorrowful connotation it bears in our culture. It was more about enduring. Suffering, or more accurately, to suffer, was less a description of a calamitous event or time and more about a people's reaction to the sorrow. Further, it was just as common for the ancients to speak of enduring the monotonous plateaus of their lives as it was to speak of enduring those occasions of profound loss.

Autumn then offered a wondrous observation around enduring. She reminded me that Jesus was "made like His brethren in all things... He Himself was tried by that which He suffered, or endured" (Hebrews 2:17–18). Then, turning the tables, she recalled that God—by monotony and adversity—strengthens our enduring, that we might "share in his holiness" (Hebrews 2:7–11).

Suffering—or enduring—then should not be regarded lightly, or become a place of surrender, or an excuse to betray a root of bitterness.

For it's a mysterious place of wonder—a place of communion even—where God partook of the nature of man and where man can partake of the nature of God.

Where is your greatest call to suffer, or to endure? Is it enduring those occasions of profound loss or enduring the monotonous plateaus? § Is there a common theme to the places that call forth your endurance? Spiritual? Emotional? Mental? Physical? Social? What does it look like? Name it. § What's a new perspective you might occupy around your distinctive themes of trial? Paul got it: "For our light and momentary troubles are achieving for us an eternal glory that far outweighs them all" (2 Corinthians 4:16–17).

SAFE AT HOME!

THE FOURTH:
GREEN CATHEDRALS

Baseball is the only sport

with the beauty and sophistication to be played on a diamond.

Unknown

THE FOURTH:
GREEN CATHEDRALS

It was another beautiful evening in Chavez Ravine, home of Dodger Stadium. The ballpark—an icon of Mid-Century Modern architecture—then as now, illuminated the night, a brilliant crown perched atop the Los Angeles skyline. On this evening a generation ago, I carried my nephews, Daniel and Kevin—perhaps four and six years old at the time—to their first Major League Baseball game, the Dodgers and the Mets. The boys were dressed in Dodger uniforms, carried homemade poster board signs, and had five dollars each to spend on souvenirs.

I don't remember my first visit to Dodger Stadium. Indeed, I can't recall a time when our family did not travel from our home in suburban Los Angeles to watch the Dodgers. Koufax and Roseboro represent the Dodgers of my childhood; Hershiser and Piazza embody the team of my nephews' youth. Although I cannot recall my first game, I saw it all anew that night through the wide eyes of Daniel and Kevin.

About the third inning the boys were ready to visit the souvenir stand, where all things Dodger Blue (Pantone 294, for you curious artists) are sold. I understand that time can exaggerate our memories, but I seem to recall that Abraham Lincoln beat Kevin to the counter. Kevin surrendered his bill to the attendant and enthusiastically purchased the first thing he saw that fell within his budget. Daniel, however, kept his president in his hip pocket. For the next several minutes he grilled the patient attendant, inquiring of numerous items in the display, "How much is that?" "How much is that?" "How much is that?" Finally, Daniel turned to me and asked, "Uncle Michael, can we come back later? I'd like to think about it for a while."

Daniel turned to me an hour later, in the seventh inning, and announced, "I'm ready to go back to the souvenir stand, Uncle Michael." When we approached the counter, Daniel—with clarity and intention—pointed out three items to the attendant and quickly said, "I'll take one of those, one of those, and one of those." Kevin looked down at his own comparatively meager purchase, then looked with disbelief at his brother's trove, and asked, "Daniel, how'd you do that?"

Daniel and Kevin are adults today, beloved brothers and successful men with their own distinctive identities and families. But it's amazing how that night long ago at the ballpark offered a glimpse of their developed personalities. Neither one, either good or bad. In Myers-Briggs parlance, Daniel is a P for Perceiving—he prefers to stay open to new information and options; Kevin is a J for Judging—he prefers to get things decided. Who knew you could discern so much from a bobblehead?

What stories of your childhood have you heard from family and friends that foreshadowed your personality preferences? § How might those preferences have served you in life—to your favor or not so much? § Can you identify an occasion when you acted out of preference? How might that have served you? § What's the learning?

I've been contemplating the tabernacle and temples of the Old and New Testaments: the seven include the natural temple of Eden and its Garden, the Tabernacle, the Temple of Solomon, the Second Temple, the person of Jesus, the people of God, and the New Jerusalem. For some, reflection on the tabernacle and temples of scripture is merely ancient history; in reality, their story is relevant to a conversation around spiritual formation.

Little remains of the two stone temples. Most prominent among the remnants is the Western Wall of the Second Temple—the Wailing Wall. The Wailing Wall is a small portion of a large retaining wall encasing the Temple Mount to support King Herod's massive expansion of the Second Temple. The Wailing Wall—because of its connection to the temple—is regarded as a holy place of prayer by the Jewish people.

• • •

At the risk of sounding foolish, baseball too has its cherished, sacred remnants.

The old "jewel box" stadiums of yesteryear have long been described as baseball's green cathedrals. Congregants—many of them dressed in their Sunday best—alternately stood up and sat down, joining their voices in common liturgical expression. They cheered their proxies on the field who heroically expended strength and sacrifice in a timeless story of leaving and returning home. The scene is not unlike the one painted by the author of Hebrews (11:1–12:3).

These classic ballparks—built between 1895 and 1923—were the first generation of stadiums constructed of steel and concrete, rather than wood. Clubs were now able to build stadiums with greater structural support that allowed multiple tiers of seating; these ballparks resembled an open jewel box with its cascading levels of compartments. Only two remain: Boston's Fenway Park and Chicago's Wrigley Field. Original Yankee Stadium—built in 1923, razed in 2008—was the last of the jewel box stadiums erected and the most recent to fall.

But, like the temple in Jerusalem, remnants of these early, green cathedrals remain—if you know where to look.

Near the corner of Third Avenue and First Street in Brooklyn, a concrete wall forms a portion of the perimeter of a ConEd storage yard. The casual pedestrian hasn't a clue that the edifice was once part of the left center field wall in Washington Park, home of the Dodgers from

BASEBALL AND OUR PILGRIMAGE HOME

1898 through 1912 ⁌ A short walk takes you to the original location of Washington Baseball Park where the Dodgers began play in 1883. Their clubhouse was in the Old Stone House built in 1699—imagine, they dressed for the game in a structure that was a witness (and, indeed, a participant) in the American Revolution. The house has been restored and is now a museum.

And there are others. In Harlem, a staircase descends mysteriously from Coogan's Bluff to the former site of the Polo Grounds—once home to the Giants and, for a time, the Yankees ⁌ A mile from Boston's Fenway Park was Braves Field—yes, those Braves. The old ticket office still stands and is occupied by the Boston University Police Department ⁌ The site of Forbes Field, home to the Pirates for sixty-one years, now belongs to its surviving neighbor, the University of Pittsburgh. Sections of Forbes' brick outfield wall have been faithfully preserved on campus. Home plate can be found in its original position, visible under a Plexiglas tile in Posvar Hall ⁌ And in Cleveland, where the Indians played in League Park until 1946, a ball field and a park have been built around the ticket office and a portion of the outfield wall that remain from the stadium.

Today, a journey to the old ballparks and their remnants has become, for many, a pilgrimage. A pilgrimage home.

• • •

Scripture, however, shows no such sentiment to the temples of stone. Temple today is within and among the people of God.

The Apostle Paul declared, "The God who made the world and all things in it, since He is Lord of heaven and earth, does not dwell in temples made with hands" (Acts 17:24); and elsewhere, "Do you not know that you yourselves are God's temple, and that God's Spirit dwells in you?" (1 Corinthians 3:16). In fact, like Jesus before, the people of God are temple, priest, and sacrifice: temple, for God dwells within them; priest, for they intercede on behalf of others; and sacrifice, for they offer their bodies as a living sacrifice for the sake of others.

How good might life be if you, as a follower of Jesus, instead of merely attending worship as a spectator, lived with intention as temple, priest, and sacrifice? § If Jesus visited your church, your neighborhood, your community, what needs would he find compelling? § Consider ways that sentiment toward the physical structures of our faith might supplant our embodiment of the faith—that is to say, we place our trust in a temple, a brick and mortar place of worship, rather than become temple.

Walk through the tunnel from the outer concourse to your seats at a Major League Baseball stadium. From the narrowing constraints of the darkened passageway, your attention is first beckoned by the blue sky at the other end; walk a few steps farther and the emerald expanse of the field bursts into view. Here in the heart of the metropolis is a field of play; its very centers—home, infield, outfield—a nod to a forgotten, centuries-old, European system of farming. The field itself—its clay and its grass; its circles and its squares—wakens something deep within, well before the players take the field and the game begins.

Baseball. It's not just pretty. It's good design.

Design that is both affective and effective—whether graphic, structural, interior, or fashion design—is more than a random composition of elements. Good design captivates our senses and our reason, our heart and our mind. Consequently, a successful designer doesn't simply, instinctively, make pretty or clever things; she rather has studied and understands how people perceive and communicate.

For this reason, professional designers and doctors of psychology have more in common than a pencil and a journal. In fact, the foundation of good design is the five key principles of a German school of psychology known as Gestalt, meaning shape or form. Gestalt fundamentally teaches that the whole is greater than the sum of its parts; that the relationships shared by the parts, and not the parts themselves, contribute to how the whole is perceived.

For example, a vintage theater marquee may feature hundreds of flashing yellow light bulbs. However, what captures the eye of the passerby is not the individual bulbs, but the perception of the lights marching in step around the perimeter of the marquee's sign board.

• • •

The five key principles of Gestalt theory of design include the following, and you can see them on the ball field:

Similarity. Similarity is when parts of the whole look alike. Because of their resemblance, the parts as a group or a pattern are often what a person perceives. (See, for example, Mitsubishi's diamonds logo.) When there is similarity a designer can interject an object that is dissimilar to the others, or an anomaly. The anomaly then becomes the focal point of the design. Similarity is in play on the ball field in the relationship between the familiar square pillows that are first, second, and third bases; home plate is the anomaly. And, in a very subtle way, similarity shows up in that most major dimensions of the ball field are divisible by the number three, a key number in the game itself.

Continuation. Continuation is when the parts of the image are arranged on a line or a curve and naturally prompt a person's eye to move through one object and to continue to another. (See, for example, Amazon's a-through-z logo.) Continuation is in play on the ball field as the left and right foul lines extend from home plate through the clay and the grass, climb the outfield walls and the foul poles, and theoretically ascend into the endless sky above.

Closure. Closure is when a form is incomplete or a space is not completely enclosed. If enough of the shape is apparent, a person's mind initially, intuitively, perceives the whole and fills in the missing information. (See, for example, NBC's peacock logo.) Closure is in play on the ball field—content with one example—in the precise arc that divides the infield from the outfield, a circle really, the center of which rests on the center of another circle, the pitcher's mound.

BASEBALL AND OUR PILGRIMAGE HOME

Proximity. Proximity is when the parts are sufficiently close together that a person tends to perceive them as one group, united as a whole. (See, for example, Bank of America's field-and-flag logo.) If the parts are placed without proximity they are perceived as separate shapes. Proximity is in play on the ball field in the infield. How many circles and squares can you count with intention, having never previously noticed them, because they are more familiar as parts of the whole?

Figure and Ground. A person's eye distinguishes a shape from its surrounding area. The shape is naturally perceived as the figure, or focus, and the surrounding area is perceived as the ground, or background. A designer can play with the figure and ground to bring clarity or interest to the whole. (Have you ever seen the arrow within the FedEx logo, or the driver in the VW logo?) Figure and ground is in play on the ball field in the clay and the grass. Which is the shape and which is the background? It may depend upon where you are looking.

• • •

Baseball. It's not just pretty. It's good design.

No other team sport—football, basketball, hockey, to name a few—rejects the sterile rectangle for the careful composition of circles and squares and lines that define a baseball's field of play. Outside of team sports, only a golf course, I confess begrudgingly, approaches at once the simplicity and complexity of a ballpark. But then golf, like t-ball, was clearly invented for those who can't hit a curveball.

Good design is everywhere; so, for that matter, is bad design. Now that you know a bit of what makes the difference between the two, become aware of the difference—on a billboard, in a logo, in the trees. § Get curious and appreciative of good design. Behind all good design is a good designer. Become aware of the Divine Designer. § And here's a final inquiry for Christ followers. Recall the meaning of Gestalt: "Gestalt fundamentally teaches that the whole is greater than the sum of its parts; that the relationships shared by the parts, and not the parts themselves, contribute to how the whole is perceived." How does Gestalt show up in the body of Christ, the church?

There's a tranquil space in the midst of Monroe, Louisiana, some twenty-five miles from our home in rural Farmerville. It's a lovely recreation area, called Forsythe Park, on the northern edge of the historic Garden District, on the eastern bank of the Ouachita River. Forsythe Park is a civic treasure that was developed at the turn of the twentieth century. I've spent many an afternoon reading 'neath the shade of its old trees or walking its footpaths around the pool, the small golf course, and the spot where once was a ball field. Ah, yes, the ball field.

I'll get back to that in a moment.

I grew up in Los Angeles, in the shadow of Dodger Stadium. The beautiful park sits atop a mountain overlooking the city. When the stadium is illuminated for a night game, it looks like a brilliant, jewel-encrusted crown on the head of a monarch surveying her kingdom. Just perhaps, her imagination drifts thousands of miles across the nation to another ball yard where her longtime rival from the Bronx reigns.

Among the most storied rivalries in our nation's sporting history is that shared by the Dodgers (est, in Brooklyn, 1883, moved to Los Angeles in 1958) and Yankees (est. in Baltimore, 1901, moved to New York City in 1903, and later to the Bronx).

The Brooklyn Dodgers and the New York Yankees first met in the World Series in 1941. They've squared off in the Series eleven times (as of 2017)—more than any other two teams. A highlight reel of World Series history would be filled with cuts featuring the two franchises:

Dodger catcher Mickey Owens' passed ball on a third strike with two out in the ninth inning of pivotal Game 4 of the '41 Series § Any one of the Fall Classics from '47 to '56, when the Dodgers' fabled Boys of Summer met the Yankees in the Series six out of ten years. The perennial battle cry of the feckless Dodgers became, "Wait 'til next year!" § In '55, when the Dodgers beat the Yankees for their first World Series title, and the mantra changed to, "This is next year!" § Don Larsen's pitcher perfect Game 5 in '56 (27 Dodgers to bat; 27 Dodgers retired with nary a base runner), a fete never equaled before or after in World Series history.

The '63 Series was the first between the foes after the Dodgers moved west and the rivalry grew from cross-town to cross-country. The Dodgers, led by aces Koufax, Drysdale, and Podres, humiliated the Yankees, sweeping the Series four games to none. The Yankees scored a total of four runs in the Series; not once in four games did the New Yorkers ever lead § (Incidentally, '63 was the only year my father invested in season tickets. He gave the tickets to Games 3 and 4 at Dodger Stadium to business associates and kept the tickets to Game 5 for our family. Game 5. Dad's timing was never quite the best.) § Then there was '77, '78, and '81. Steinbrenner, Lasorda, Martin, Jackson, et al. Loud, contentious, arrogant. New York prevailed two out of three.

Yankees. Dodgers. Men playing ball in baseball's great cathedrals.

But, back to that forgotten ball field in Monroe, Louisiana's Forsythe Park. Nearly a century ago, the New York Yankees and the Brooklyn Dodgers had left their Spring Training facilities in New Orleans and Clearwater, Florida, respectively. The two teams were traveling by train through the South playing exhibition games before heading north for Opening Day.

When Monroe city officials heard that the train carrying the two clubs would be passing through their city, traveling from Vicksburg to Dallas, they implored league officials to add Monroe to their schedule. The financial demands of the ball clubs were met: the teams would receive 75% of the gate with a guarantee of $250.00.

On Thursday, April 5th, 1923, Babe Ruth and his Yankee teammates and Zach Wheat and his fellow Dodgers played big league baseball before nearly four thousand spectators in the modest environs of Forsythe Park in Monroe, Louisiana.

As I sit in the quiet park this day, not even my imagination is that good.

NEW YORK YANKEES vs. BROOKLYN DODGERS
Monroe, LA • April 1923

New York	AB	R	H	RBI	Brooklyn	AB	R	H	RBI
Witt cf	5	0	1	1	Barber cf	4	0	2	1
McNally 3b	6	2	2	0	Johnston ss	5	0	0	0
Ruth rf	4	3	1	1	Griffith rf	4	0	0	0
Pipp 1b	5	1	3	1	Wheat lf	4	1	2	0
Meusel lf	5	1	1	1	Neis lf	1	0	0	0
Schang c	3	1	0	0	Schleibner 1b	5	0	2	1
Ward 2b	4	0	1	0	Bailey 2b	4	1	0	0
Tucker*	1	0	0	0	Mullen 3b	3	1	1	0
Wight 2b	0	0	0	0	DeBerry c	2	0	0	0
Scott ss	4	1	1	1	Taylor c	2	0	1	2
Shawkey p	3	0	2	0	Grimes p	2	1	1	0
Smith**	1	0	1	0	Dickerman p	2	0	0	0
Pennock p	0	0	0	0					
Totals	41	9	13	5	Totals	38	4	9	4

* Batted for Ward in 8th.
** Batted for Shawkey in 7th.

```
New York ..................  2 0 1   0 0 0   5 0 1   9
Brooklyn ..................  0 0 0   0 1 2   1 0 0   4
```

Sacrifice hits: Scott, Pennock. **2B**–Schleibner, Grimes, Mullen, McNally, Wheat, Pipp. **Team LOB**–New York 12. Brooklyn 11. **BB**–Off Grimes, 4. Off Dickerman, 1. Off Shawkey, 3. Off Pennock, 1. **Ks**–By Grimes, 2. By Dickerman, 4. By Shawkey, 5. By Pennock 4. **Wild Pitch**–Grimes. **Pitching**–7 hits, 3 runs off Shawkey in six innings; 2 hits, 1 run off Pennock in 3 innings; 4 hits, 3 runs off Grimes in 5 innings; 9 hits, 6 runs off Dickerman in four innings. **Umpires**–McGowan and Klem **T**–2:25. **A**–3,571.

**Game played on
Thursday, April 5th, 1923, at Forsythe Park, Monroe, LA**

SAFE AT HOME!

The learning from the story—if you insist I have one—is compelling. If I could travel back in time to address the Yankees and Dodgers prior to their taking the field in Monroe, ninety-odd years ago, here's what I think I'd say, "You fellows have no idea just how big Major League Baseball and the Dodgers and the Yankees are destined to become. Imagine it. Inhabit it. Now. Oh, and Mr. Ruth and Mr. Wheat. Would you both kindly sign baseballs and send them in a weather-proof box, to General Delivery, Farmerville, Louisiana. Instruct them to hold them until December 15th, 2017." If I could address the Yankees and Dodgers of the modern era, I think I'd say, "In humility, honor your roots." Sound advice to all.

POSTSCRIPT: 1923 would prove to be a banner year for the Yankees. On April 18th—not quite two weeks after their visit to Forsythe Park in Monroe—the Yankees opened the season in their new ballpark. Babe Ruth, naturally, hit the first home run in the new stadium on Opening Day, April 18th; eventually, the new stadium acquired the moniker, The House that Ruth Built ⊏ Later that year, on June 15th, Lou Gehrig signed with the Yankees out of Columbia University, and appeared in his first Major League Baseball Game. He'd play ball seventeen years—nearly half his thirty-eight years and exclusively for the Yankees—before ALS cut short his career and his life ⊏ Still later that same year, the Yankees won the first of twenty-seven World Series titles, besting the New York Giants, four games to two.

BASEBALL AND OUR PILGRIMAGE HOME

"Life begins on Opening Day," baseball writer Tom Boswell once penned. In honor of this year's Opening Day Weekend, I'd like to share with you two anecdotes from baseball, including one from my own experience, that share a common learning.

First, baseball legend Joe DiMaggio and film star Marilyn Monroe were married in San Francisco on January 14th, 1954. Joe and Marilyn were of opposite temperaments: she hungered for the crowds and attention that he found distasteful.

While on their honeymoon in Tokyo, Marilyn took a side trip to entertain the troops in Korea. Upon her return to Tokyo, she told Joe of the exuberant crowds: "Joe," she said, "you never heard such cheering." Dispirited, Joe replied, "Yes, I have."

Second, several years ago I had a conversation with Jack Sanford, pitcher for the Philadelphia Phillies, San Francisco Giants, and Kansas City Athletics. Jack was Rookie of the Year in 1957 with the Phillies and finished second to Don Drysdale in the Cy Young Award voting in 1962 with the Giants. He spoke of his experience pitching for the Giants against the Yankees in Game 7 of the 1962 World Series. Jack lost the game by inches when Yankees second baseman Bobby Richardson caught Willie McCovey's line drive with runners on second and third bases in the ninth inning. A foot or two in either direction and McCovey would have won the game and the series for Sanford and the Giants.

I asked Jack, "When you were on the mound in the ninth inning of the seventh game of the World Series, did you have any consciousness that you were living every little boy's dream?" Jack looked at me for a moment, his eyes moist with tears, and he answered, "I wish you were my wife."

Many men and women of accomplishment, like Joe DiMaggio and Jack Sanford, find it difficult when those closest to them neither understand nor appreciate their experiences and accomplishments. It can prove lonesome.

What experience or accomplishment do you hold close to your breast that you wish you could fully celebrate with those closest to you? § How would their knowing help you feel more fully known? § What personal, compelling value might that experience or accomplishment represent?

On Monday and Tuesday, September 15th and 16th of 2008, I joined my nephews—Kevin from Midland, Texas along with his then three-year old son Andrew, and Daniel from Los Angeles, California—at old Yankees Stadium in New York. We converged upon the Bronx for two games of the final week in the life of the grand dame of ballparks before her collapse that winter. On Tuesday morning, Daniel returned to law school at UCLA; his seat was filled for the second game by Jackson, a young boy from my church in Auburn, California.

BASEBALL AND OUR PILGRIMAGE HOME

I've previously written of this baseball pilgrimage; this, however, is the story of how Jackson joined me, my nephews, and my great nephew for a magical night of baseball in New York City.

A scant two weeks before our trip, Jackson—a young man whom I had known all of his eleven years—quietly approached me at worship and asked, "Uncle Michael, is it true you're going to a game at Yankee Stadium?" I replied with a smile, "No, Jack, I'm going to two games at Yankee Stadium. What do you think of that?" Jackson stared at his shoes and quietly, half-heartedly, replied, "Cool." He then asked, "Will you bring me a pennant?"

Jack's melancholy resonated with my spirit. When I was his age, a handful of ancient stadiums closed to make way for a generation of monolithic, multi-purpose, indistinct, concrete stadiums that were erected in the 1970s and 80s. Forbes Field in Pittsburgh, Crosley Field in Cincinnati, Shibe Park in Philadelphia, Commiskey Park in Chicago all returned to the dust from whence they came. A significant era was passing before my young eyes. And I watched helplessly from afar with nary a chance of walking their historic concourses, immersing myself in the sights and sounds and smells and flavors of an historic ballpark—baseball's version of a seasoned cast iron skillet.

Within the next couple of days, Kathy had a conversation with Jackson's mother. She told Kathy that Jackson had been grieving for months—even at times expressing anger around—the loss of Yankee Stadium. It was inexplicable. His parents had no interest in baseball.

I had no idea that Jackson, in measure, shared my strong connection to the history of baseball and its icons.

Knowing we had a spare ticket for Tuesday's game, Kathy and I approached Jackson's parents with the possibility of his flying to New York overnight Monday to attend Tuesday's game. We agreed not to tell Jackson until his parents were sure they could arrange his travel.

On the Thursday before my Sunday departure, we finally received word that Jackson had a flight to New York. That evening, Kathy and I visited Jackson. He still had no knowledge of what was about to happen. I told Jackson, "I've felt bad that you're unable to see Yankee Stadium before it comes down. Kathy and I would like you to have this memento." I handed Jackson an envelope. Within the envelope was a replica I had prepared of his game ticket and a card with a rather abrupt message, "Buy your own pennant!"

Jack carefully, cautiously pulled the card from the envelope. He looked at us, then at his parents, confused by the message on the card. I said, "Jack, there's something else in the envelope." Jack reached down into the envelope and withdrew the faux ticket. There was quiet as he vacantly stared at the treasure. Finally, I softly said, "Jack, next Tuesday, God willing, you'll be sitting next to me at Yankee Stadium." He looked around at the others in the room, without word or expression. After several moments, Kathy said, "Jackson, breathe!" He looked at Kathy. He looked at me. He looked at his parents. The corners of his mouth began to turn up in a subdued smile. Then he collapsed into my arms, sobbing.

BASEBALL AND OUR PILGRIMAGE HOME

The following Tuesday night, we witnessed a record that will never be broken. Yankees legend Derek Jeter—with just a few games left to manage it—broke baseball immortal Lou Gehrig's record for most career hits in Yankees Stadium. The ovation Jeter received was deafening. But even more memorable to me of that now distant night in New York City was the opportunity I had—with the help of others—to fulfill the dream of a young boy.

Have you ever had the opportunity to fulfill the dream of another? § How might fulfilling the dream of another be a reflection of divine grace? § Where's a present opportunity for you to show grace to another?

Tug McGraw—primarily known today as the late father of country singer Tim McGraw—was a renown, and colorful, relief pitcher for the New York Mets from 1965 to 1974. During one difficult outing, his equally colorful manager, legendary Casey Stengel, came to remove him from the game. McGraw begged Casey to leave him in for just one more batter, saying, "I know I can get this next guy out, I've already gotten him out twice." To which Casey replied, "Yeah, but it was earlier in this inning."

Which leads me to recall another meeting on a mound centuries ago (Luke 9:18–62).

SAFE AT HOME!

• • •

It was six months prior to the cross. Jesus and his apostles were north of Jerusalem, in proximity to the coastal city of Caesarea Philippi, far removed from the urban centers of opposition. The week before had started with promise, when the Apostle Peter answered Jesus' question—"Who do people say I am?—by unequivocally declaring, "You are the Messiah, the Son of the Living God." Within days, however, as Jesus intensified efforts to prepare the twelve for his death, Peter unwittingly cast an old stumbling block before Jesus, assuring him, "Never, Lord! This shall never happen to you!" By week's end, Jesus' spirit was struggling in anticipation of his Passion.

Accompanied by Peter, James, and John, Jesus ascended a mountain to pray. Day turned into night; exhaustion overcame the three apostles; yet, still, Jesus prayed. As he prayed, two familiar figures from Israel's storied past—Moses and Elijah, representing the Law and the Prophets—joined Jesus on the mound.

The three heroes of faith, transfigured "in glorious splendor" against the canopy of darkness, talked amongst themselves.

• • •

All of which reminds me of a summer afternoon, half a lifetime ago, at Dodger Stadium in Los Angeles. I was walking an empty concourse near the Press Box when I passed two elderly gentlemen, followed by their wives and engaged in quiet conversation. As we passed in the hall, I recognized them as baseball pioneers Casey Stengel and Babe Herman.

I remember thinking to myself, "What do my baseball heroes talk about amongst themselves?"

While I can't tell you what was on the minds of Misters Stengel and Herman, we're not left to wonder of Jesus, Moses, and Elijah's conversation. "They spoke about Jesus' departure, which he was about to bring to fulfillment at Jerusalem."

The words Moses and Elijah spoke to encourage Jesus on the mound proved effective. Any timidity was transformed into tenacity, any fear into faith; and from that moment, "...as the time approached for him to be taken up to heaven, Jesus resolutely set out for Jerusalem."

A meeting on the mound can change the direction of the game.

What comes up for you when you consider the possibility that Jesus struggled within as he contemplated his Passion? § How was this struggle essential to equip Jesus to become our merciful and faithful high priest? (Hebrews 2:14–18). § Explain how Moses and Elijah, though certainly empathetic to his fears, might not have been entirely objective in their conversation with Jesus. § If you find yourself in trouble, who would you summon to meet you on the mound? What might they say to you this very day?

SAFE AT HOME!

THE FIFTH:
6 + 4 + 3 = 2

Ninety feet between home plate and first base
may be the closest man has ever come to perfection.

Red Smith

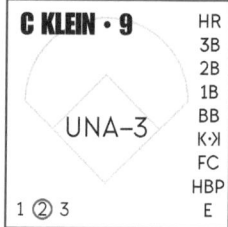

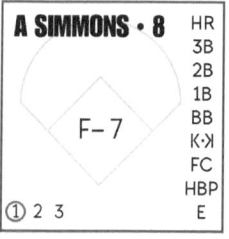

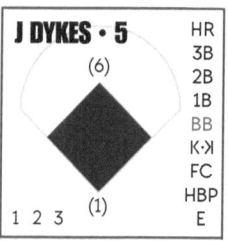

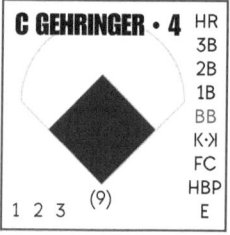

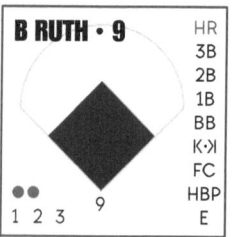

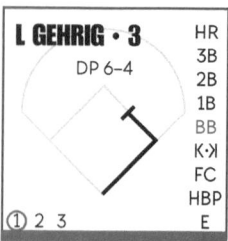

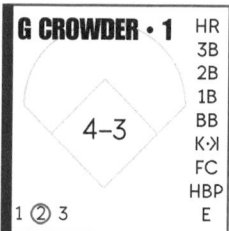

THE FIFTH:

6 + 4 + 3 = 2

Of the many curious commonalities shared by the Creator and Cooperstown is the custom of counting on characters. You see, scripture assigns meaning to numbers. The numbers 3, 7, 10, and 12, for example, are numbers of perfection. The number 3 represents the Godhead: Father, Son, and Spirit. The number 7 is foundational in scripture. It's the number of the creation week. The Apostle John used the number 7 to organize his two masterworks, The Gospel of John and The Revelation.

The number 10 represents completion. Think Ten Commandments. Append two zeroes to the number ten and you have 1,000, a number that compounds the completion represented by 10. To borrow a baseball term, 1,000 is 10 on steroids. The number 1,000 looms large in The Revelation. Additionally, the infamous judge, Samson, is said to have killed 1,000 men with the jawbone of an ass. I fear the same weapon has injured countless more throughout the centuries. And, of course, the number 12—also a number of completion—is the number both of the tribes of Israel in the Old Testament and of the apostles in the New. And don't get me started on the completion represented by 144,000, which is 12 x (12 x 1,000).

Baseball, too, as the reader will discover, is built on the back of the number 3. Nearly every number essential to the game is a multiple of 3. (Except for that pesky variant, 4 balls, when the batter is awarded a free pass to first base. Perhaps the number 4 was intended as a humiliation to the errant pitcher, suggesting, "Look, we've given you an extra opprtunity to get the fellow out and you still failed.")

Numbers, in fact, are used in baseball to record the story of a baseball game. Each position is assigned a number: the pitcher, naturally, is assigned 1; a catcher—perhaps with a nod to his squat—is assigned the number 2; numbers 3–6 represent the first baseman, secondbaseman, third baseman, and shortstop, respectively; and the outfielders are assigned numbers 7, 8, and 9, moving left to right. A scorekeeper would thus use the notation "1–3" for a ground out fielded by the pitcher and thrown to the first baseman. A fly out to right field merits F–9. And, 6–4–3 is a ground out double play from short to second to first. And, further, numbers are used to measure the performance and value of those who play the game. Numbers count in baseball.

BASEBALL AND OUR PILGRIMAGE HOME

I want to write about sac 9·, but, first, a little context might be helpful. Yes, it's about baseball—and, ultimately, about life.

First, baseball is—as is The Divine Narrative of scripture—an unfolding and unanticipated, sometimes chaotic, drama of reconciliation and redemption—a Homeresque story of leaving and returning home. The individual and the team. Law and grace. Hits and misses. Runs and errors. Players enter and leave a game's narrative, never to return.

Second, baseball is timeless; there's no clock in baseball. In fact, as if in spite of the clock and time itself, the game of baseball moves around the bases counterclockwise. A baseball game could, in theory, extend without end into extra innings. James Penrice, author of *Crossing Home*, has observed: "Just outside the stadium walls buses are operating on schedules, workers are punching clocks, kitchen timers are running, alarm clocks are being set. Yet inside these walls players and fans have crossed into a dimension where time disappears, where our finite world and world of the infinite cross" (p. 28).

And, third, only baseball chronicles each game so methodically that a game's narrative can be relived, unedited, from the scorecard. A scorecard employs an elegant shorthand—simple enough for a child to grasp, comprehensive enough for a statistician to employ—to record every detail of a game.

Which brings us to the significance of sac 9·.

SAFE AT HOME!

This simple notation from a baseball scorecard—though isolated from its context—yields remarkable detail. The game's score is close, perhaps in the late innings. At least one runner's on base, most likely at third. There are less than two out in the inning. The batter lifts a fly ball deep to right field. The ball's swallowed up by the fielder's glove; the runner at third sprints home and slides into the plate amidst a cloud of dust, just before the ball, hurled from right field, finds its mark in the catcher's glove. All under the wary eye of the pitcher, who's standing between the catcher and the backstop, just in case.

But, oddly enough, this post isn't about scoring. It's about sacrifice...

Jesus said, "I tell you the truth, unless a kernel of wheat is planted in the soil and dies, it remains alone... Those who love their life in this world will lose it. Those who care nothing for their life in this world will keep it for eternity" (John 12:24–25, NLT). Paul testified of Jesus, "... have the same mindset as Christ Jesus: who, being in very nature God, did not consider equality with God something to be used to his own advantage; rather, he made himself nothing by taking the very nature of a servant..." (Philippians 2:5-8, NIV).

In baseball—as in The Divine Narrative—the sacrifice of the one for the many is honored as virtue; indeed, among all sports, only baseball statistically recognizes the value of sacrifice—in the form of either a fly ball to the outfield or a bunt to the infield. To paraphrase an anonymous scribe, if the home run is the heroic muscle of baseball, the sacrifice is its self-effacing soul. As one has said, "Greater love has no one than this, that one lay down a bunt for his friends." That's a paraphrase, but you get the message.

How much might you rely upon personality and power, rather than character and presence? § Why is a reliance upon personality and power a difficult place from which to live? § What does sacrifice look like to you? How does it show up in your life? Or not? § Where's the place to forward and deepen the learning?

A baseball scorecard shares secrets with those who are proficient in its language and who are passionate for the game. For instance, did you know, one team's scorecard can often identify the style of the opposing pitcher. If ground balls accounted for more than half of a team's offensive outs, the opposing pitcher was most likely a control artist whose pitches break, or drop, into the lower half of the strike zone; and these pitches would include sinkers and splitters. If, however, a team's scorecard is riddled with Ks (strikeouts; by "riddled," I mean at least one strikeout per inning pitched) and BBs (base on balls, or walks)—the opposing pitcher was most likely a velocity, or power, pitcher who predominantly throws fastballs, change-ups, and curves.

But, it wasn't my intent to talk about baseball.

There is, however, a connection between baseball and the point of this piece. Baseball is often called a game of numbers; the New Testament's Revelation is often called a book of numbers. While numbers can be counted on in The Revelation, don't try to perform math on them. Numbers in The Revelation are strictly used metaphorically.

Take, for example, that infamous number 666, the number ascribed to the dragon.

Come, now, there was no need for you to dive in horror under the table. Seriously, come out from under the table and pay attention.

The dragon of The Revelation did not personally adopt 666 as his nickname and have it embroidered on the back of his worn, black leather jacket. The Spirit of God coined the term, and he did not intend for the tag to bolster the lore of the dragon or to summon images of unspeakable terror in the hearts of the readers of The Revelation. 666 is actually something of a derisive term intended to express the limits of the dragon's power.

Think of it this way. Imagine a decimal point after the first 6. The number now reads 6.66. By contrast, the number of the divine in The Revelation is 7. It doesn't matter how many sixes you add after the decimal, the number will never reach seven. In other words, no matter how bad the dragon grows, he can never be as bad as God is good.

Back to baseball for the final point.

Often when a velocity pitcher is mowing down the opposition, striking out one batter after another, you'll see fans in the bleachers triumphantly post a large paper K on the outfield wall. One K for each strikeout. I think of those paper Ks when I hear of evil in the world. A child is abused. The dragon gets another 6. A terrorist attack robs the innocent of life. The dragon gets another 6. The Giants win another pennant. The dragon gets another 6.

The dragon—no matter how many additional 6s are posted—will never reach 7 in power.

He can never be as bad as God is good.

666, then, feels a bit like a promise, doesn't it?

How would your life change, if you stopped believing the dragon's own press releases? § What's the learning, in context of this piece, of James' assurance: "Resist the devil and he will flee from you. Draw near to God and He will draw near to you" (James 4:7–8).

A successful man or woman is one who knows how to fail with success. To illustrate, it's back to baseball. For the three of you out there who don't appreciate the nuances of the game, endure to the end for a powerful spiritual learning.

• • •

First, a bit of context. When I started collecting baseball cards in my single digits, I spent endless hours digesting the wealth of data on the back of those cardboard squares. A 1968 card of a position player (that is, anyone other than a pitcher) featured a modest menu of traditional but, in some cases, dubious statistics including At Bats (AB), Hits (H), Doubles (2B), Triples (3B), Home Runs (HR), Runs Batted In (RBI), and Batting Average (AVG). A pitcher's card from that same year long ago included Wins (W), Losses (L), Percentage (PCT), Strikeouts (SO), Bases on Balls (BB), and that curious Earned Run Average (ERA).

These are the numbers by which a player's performance and, therefore, value were measured and judged. These are the numbers—in some cases quite flawed—by which the value of one player was compared to the value of another. These are the numbers which, at least in part, determined a man's livelihood and, in the end, earned an invitation from the club to retire.

But, prior to the 2015 season, Major League Baseball developed and installed in all thirty stadiums a proprietary system of data collection and analysis called Statcast. Statcast employs a series of high-resolution optical cameras and radar equipment that precisely tracks the movements of the ball and every player on the field. (Curiously, baseball has never been on the cutting edge of technology; and, ironically, two of the thirty stadiums where Statcast is installed still use manually operated scoreboards.)

What can Statcast track on the field? The full possibilities have yet to be imagined. Here are a few present uses:

One, Statcast can measure the spin rate of a baseball from the time the pitcher releases it until it thuds into the leather of the catcher's mitt. If the number of rotations begins to decrease, the manager can tell the pitcher is starting to tire—well before he gives up a game-winning hit to the opposition.

Two, Statcast can measure the velocity, launch angle, and vector of a batted ball; it can track the hang time and distance a ball travels and can project the landing spot of a home run. Consequently, hitters can use Statcast during a game to adjust the angle of their swing to give the ball the best chance of leaving the yard.

Three, Statcast can track what previously could not be measured. It can determine how far a fielder will range from his set position to make a defensive play on the fly; how efficient his route was on a given play while tracking a fly ball; and the velocity of his throw back to the infield.

• • •

Which—finally, you'll say—returns us to the point of the essay: a successful man or woman is one who knows how to fail with success. Statcast actually established what the best baseball minds had intuited for years. Flawlessness is rarely a mark of the successful elite, either on the ball field or in any field. There have always been players with high, nearly perfect, Fielding Percentage numbers from year to year; that is to say, they've committed few, if any, errors within a season. Statcast proved that, in some cases, these virtually flawless fielders intentionally limit their defensive range to a restricted area. They rarely, if ever, take a chance, risk an error, to be—yes, I know, but I'll say it anyway—outstanding in their field.

Where in life do you tend to avoid risk for fear of failure? Here's a question worthy of your contemplation...Where do you avoid risk for fear of what you might lose? Now, where is the greatest potential loss: in trying, but failing; or in not trying at all? § Who do you know who seems to have a rather cavalier attitude toward success and failure? What questions would you like to ask him/her? Now, set up the interview! What's the learning?

POSTSCRIPT: It's not clear why baseball, from the outset, made accommodation in the rules for an error. Bill James, baseball's legendary statistical researcher and author, once wrote of the error: "It is without exception, the only major statistic in sports, which is a record of what an observer thinks should have been accomplished." The observer who has the authority to rebrand a hit as an error or an error as a hit is the game's official scorer. The scorer is paid $150.00/per game. Imagine. The scorer—who presumably has a passion for the game of baseball but not the talent to play at the highest level—earns $150.00/game and has the authority to bring judgment upon a professional ballplayer who, on average, earns a bit under $25,000/per game. Where else in life do those with so much to envy sit in judgment of those who are living their shared dream?

BASEBALL AND OUR PILGRIMAGE HOME

Our world is the ordered creation of a Divine Designer. And, as in the case of all great creatives, God's unique personality and preferences infuse his art. We observe, for example, evidence of the Divine, or Golden, Ratio throughout the natural world. (It's worth looking up!) Again, we observe, as our eyes sweep across land and sky, we see nature awash in hues of blue and green—evidence that God is drawn to that third of his color wheel. And, yet again, we observe, in another of God's masterworks, the scriptures, a partiality to the number three.

God's favorite number? The number three looms large in scripture; here's but a sampling.... Father, Son, Spirit... body, soul, spirit... justice, lovingkindness, humility.... Moses, Elijah, Jesus transfigured and witnessed by Peter, James, John... The essential gospel: [one] Christ died for our sins; [two] He was buried; [three] He was raised on the third day... Jesus, prophet, priest, king... God, Him who is, who was, who is to come"...and countless others.

Now, it would be natural to assume that the creative work of men and women—sons and daughters of the Divine Designer; his creative apprentices—is naturally influenced, even unawares, by the Master's predilections. And, indeed, there is a latent recognition within us of the significance of the number three, as if something in our DNA smiles at something intangible that, for no other apparent reason, feels innately familiar or comfortable or even safe.

Allow me to offer but one example of the preeminence of the number three from among the work of humanity. Oh, just a random example.

I know, let's use baseball, as a case in point.

Of baseball and the number three. Baseball, it's been said, is a game of numbers. True. But what is most true is that baseball is a game of a number. For the number three is the foundation upon which the entire game was designed. And therein lies a reflection of the Divine.

It's everywhere in baseball. The number three.

Baseball's field has three distinct spaces, imported from an archaic system of farming: home, infield, and outfield. There are three outfielders, three basemen, three bases. Three strikes, you're out; three outs, you're out—back in the field.

Babe Ruth—the man-child who, arguably, saved baseball following the 1919 Black Sox scandal; changed the way baseball was played offensively; and, became the most popular player ever to play the game, Babe Ruth—wore the number three on the back of his uniform.

The examples multiply, literally. Three times three equals nine. Baseball is a game of nine innings. There are nine positions on the field. (No wonder the tenth man, the designated hitter, feels like an intrusion thrust upon the game.) There are ninety feet between bases. There are precisely 108 (yet another multiple of 3) stitches of red thread on every baseball.

Three's a crowd. To be fair, the number three can show up on a ball field even in unexpected ways. One of the most inglorious examples took place on August 15th, 1926, when the Brooklyn Dodgers hosted the Boston Braves at Ebbets Field.

The Dodgers had the bases loaded; that's three men on, for you thick-headed football fans. Babe Herman hit a line drive to right field. The base runners initially assumed the ball would be caught, and so briefly hesitated on the base paths; but, the ball bounced off the wall for a certain double. Hank DeBerry broke from third and scored. Dazzy Vance, from second base rounded third intending to score, saw the right fielder's throw to the plate, and retreated to third base. Chuck Fewster raced from first to third. And Babe Herman, bless his soul—not content with a double and oblivious to what was unfolding on the base paths—lowered his head, heroically quickened his pace, and slid fearlessly into third amidst a cloud of dust.

When the air cleared, the Dodgers had no less than three men—Fewster, Vance, and Herman—standing on third.

Shades of The Transfiguration. The Dodgers' Three-on-Third escapade became the stuff of lore in Brooklyn. It's reported some years later that a passing motorist leaned out his car window and hollered to a fan sitting in the back of Ebbets Field's grandstand, "Hey, what's the score?" "We're losing two to one," the fan replied, "last of the eighth, but we've got three men on base." To which the cynical driver replied, "Which base?"

Three beyond the ball field. But, the number three, of course, is not limited to baseball. Have you ever, for example, heard a joke about the minister, the priest, and the rabbi?... recited a nursery rhyme featuring the butcher, the baker, and the candlestick-maker?... seen a game show that asks contestants to choose one among three curtains?... heard a speaker support her thesis with three points?... seen the many Seinfeld episodes featuring three distinct story lines that intertwine, then converge with hilarity, and are resolved—all within the space of twenty-two minutes?... noticed that new car dealers often display precisely three models in their showrooms?

It can be difficult to see the forest for the threes. But, it's a start.

Now, look around. Can you identify evidence of any other of God's stylistic preferences from the natural world or from the scriptures? Can you then think of examples of how these preferences show up in the creative work of men and women—his artistic apprentices?

These are no less than the imprints of the Divine Designer upon his creation.

In 1939, the Cincinnati Reds and the New York Yankees met in the World Series. It was a different era back then. The clubs' rosters were filled with men whose names included Wally, Nino, Frenchy, Willard, Ernie, Junior, Bucky, Babe (no, another one), Lefty, Bump, and Red (two of them, actually). They were men who lived in the neighborhood and worked in their communities during the offseason.

The Yankees entered the Series as defending champions—for the third year in a row. Missing from the Yankees' roster was Lou Gehrig. This was the first season since 1923 that Gehrig had not joined the Yankees for postseason play. The "Iron Horse," his body betrayed by ALS, pulled himself from the line-up on May 2nd after playing in 2,130 consecutive games. The transitioning Bronx Bombers featured a young man from the San Francisco Bay Area—having debuted in 1936—Joe DiMaggio.

This was the Reds' first appearance in the Series since 1919 when, according to some, they were gifted the World Series Championship by members of the opposing Chicago White Sox. Eight members of the Black Sox—as that team would forever be branded—were accused, but not convicted, of throwing the Series in exchange for money paid by an infamous gambler. The Reds hoped to win an untainted championship.

The Yankees, however, were too much for the Reds. The men of the Bronx swept the Reds in four games. The final game was the Reds to lose, which they did in the ninth and tenth frames. The Yankees scored three runs in the top of the tenth to break open the game. The inning is a part of World Series folklore owing to catcher Ernie "The Schnozz" Lombardi who was stunned in a collision at the plate and allowed the Yankees to score an additional run. Sportswriters crafted an unfortunate storyline that remains nearly a century later: "The Schnozz snoozed."

• • •

The 1939 World Series was remembered today following the eighteen inning affair in Game Three of the 2018 World Series. The Dodgers beat the Red Sox in Los Angeles, 3–2, with a walk-off home run by Max Muncey. A name that might have fit better on a 1939 roster.

Game Three alone of the 2018 World Series lasted seven hours, twenty minutes. In the 1939 Series, the total playing time for the four games was seven hours, five minutes.

• • •

Game Three of the 2018 Fall Classic will likely be remembered long after other details of the Series have been forgotten. The numbers garnered in the game were remarkable and, in many cases (*), record-breaking. The game was the longest contest in World Series history, both in elapsed time (7:20*) and in number of innings (18*). The Dodgers and Red Sox used a total of 46 players.* Two pitchers from each team were even used as pinchitters.

Each team used 9 pitchers, and the 18 hurlers* threw a total of 561 pitches.* The Dodgers struck out 19 batters.* There were more combined strikeouts (34*) than hits (18), a reflection of the season itself when, for the first time in MLB history, strikeouts (41,207) outnumbered hits (41,019). Boston's Nathan Eovaldi threw 97 pitches in relief.* There were 118 at-bats.* The first four players in the Sox line-up went a combined 0 for 28.*

There were two breaks to sing Take Me Out to the Ball Game"—one in the middle of the seventh inning and one in the middle of the fourteenth inning.

• • •

But, there was something about the game that transcended the numbers, something the box score is incapable of revealing. At some point around the wild thirteenth inning, the tenor of the game changed and recalled the spirit of baseball from decades past. The ball players no longer looked like inaccessible multimillionaires cautiously playing a child's game. They looked more like the players of previous generations who often rode the subway or walked to the park in the company of their fans. They were exhausted, but immersed in the experience. They seemed to play with a sense of camaraderie alongside their teammates; of respect for their opponents; and of gratitude for the opportunity to live out every young boy's dream.

It was historic. It was terrific.

WAR. Oh, come now, it's not what you think. WAR is an acronym for a statistical measure—one among several, relatively new, mathematical equations—designed to gauge the comparative value of a Major League Baseball player. WAR stands for Wins Above Replacement. WAR calculates how many additional wins a player contributes to his team—in contrast to a replacement player of average production.

In 2017, the Houston Astros' Jose Altuve—who redefines small ball at 5'6," 165 lbs.—led the Majors among position players with a WAR of 8.3; the Cleveland Indians' Corey Kluber led the Majors among pitchers with a WAR of 8.0.* The Astros and Indians then, theoretically, each would have suffered eight additional losses had the roster spots of Misters Altuve and Kluber been instead occupied with players of average production.

By the way, the Yankees' Babe Ruth is far and away the career leader among position players with a WAR of 183.7. Think on that: 183.7. Cleveland's Cy Young is the career leader among pitchers with a WAR of 168.5. Small wonder that Ruth and Young were among the initial inductees into The National Baseball Hall of Fame at Cooperstown, New York in 1936 and 1937.

If you are not an aficionado of all things math—and I do mean all things math, for it is complicated—there is a shortcut to discover a Major League Baseball player's WAR. Flip over a Topps baseball card from the past few years; there you'll find a player's WAR alongside his more traditional statistics.

WAR can be used to compare a player's value, one, with their own performance from other seasons; two, with the performance of other players currently in the league; and, three, with the performance of iconic players of another era.

WAR, in reality, is simply a quantifiable expression of a player's Margin of Excellence. But, I'm guessing, in the world of competitive sports, the Influencers thought it more becoming of a man to speak of his WAR, than of his MoE.

Aside from financial ability, an employee or contractor is compensated, largely, according to the ease or difficulty of replacing him or her.

Imagine, if you had your own WAR: Wins Above Replacement; what in all candor, would it look like? Your WAR might not be a number; it might be descriptive of qualities, a sort of "WAR of Words."

If you were to plot your employment performance along a line that ranged from Begrudgingly Satisfy Expectations (0) to Graciously Prove Indispensable (10), where would you place yourself? What three words would you use to describe your attitude and ambition on the spectrum, if you fell somewhere between (0) and (10)? What might you do to move up a notch or two?

Identify the skills, the spirit, the strengths—the Margin of Excellence—you bring to your employer or clients; what would they include? How might you continue to develop and exercise your Margin of Excellence, and make yourself irreplaceable?

* According to Baseball-Reference.com. Each source of research on WAR in MLB uses a proprietary formula; therefore, results do vary.

Any time Dodgers baseball broadcasting legend Vin Scully declared, "Deuces are wild!," you knew something exciting might be in the offing.

"Deuces are wild!," was Scully shorthand for two out, two runners on base, a two-balls and two-strikes count on the batter. On Planet

Baseball, two on, two out, two balls, two strikes means the man at the plate and the runners on base have nothing to lose and everything to gain on the next pitch. I can virtually guarantee what will happen on the next pitch. The runners will break the moment the pitcher releases the ball. The pitcher will cut the plate in half with a fastball. The batter will do everything possible to put the ball in play. If he connects—even for a long single—the runners, given their early break, will likely score before the outfielder can return the ball to the infield.

Deuces are wild... On the afternoon of August 17th, 1957, Alice Roth brought her two grandsons to watch the Philadelphia Phillies play the visiting New York Giants. Alice was the wife of Earl Roth, an editor for the Philadelphia Bulletin newspaper. During the game, Phillies' future Hall of Fame slugger Richie Ashburn fouled a baseball into the stands. The errant foul ball struck Mrs. Roth, on the fly, in her face, breaking her nose.

The game was paused as medics stabilized the bloodied woman and prepared to remove her from the stands on a stretcher. Play resumed as the medics carried Mrs. Roth up the aisle toward the concourse. Ashburn stepped back into the batter's box and immediately fouled the first pitch he saw into the stands. Again. And, incredibly, the ball found Mrs. Roth a second time—hitting her as she was carried out on the stretcher. The second strike broke a bone in her knee.

Deuces are wild... Since 1871, less than 20,000 men have played Major League Baseball. Of those nearly 20,000 players, less than 150 have hit a career total 300 home runs or more—that's less than one player for every one hundred who have played the game. Remarkable, then, are the events of April 13th, 2009, when the Detroit Tigers hosted the Chicago White Sox.

Jermaine Dye of the Sox led off the second inning by belting a 2-1 pitch over the left-center field fence. It was a milestone. It was the 300th home run of Dye's career. The next batter, Dye's teammate Paul Konerko, stepped to the plate. Konerko connected for a home run, hitting a full-count pitch over the left-field fence. Back-to-back homeruns. And, it too was a milestone. It was the 300th home run of Konerko's career. Back-to-back three hundredth career home runs.

Deuces are wild... On April 4th, 1982, Joel Youngblood of the New York Mets played a day game against Chicago's Cubs at Wrigley Field. Youngblood had a single and two RBIs in the Mets' 7–4 victory. Following the game, Youngblood was traded to the Montreal Expos; he immediately caught a flight to Philadelphia where the Expos were playing the Phillies that evening. In the seventh inning of his personal doubleheader, Youngblood entered the game as a pinch hitter, and singled in the 5–4 loss to the Phils. Joel Youngblood is the only player in Major League Baseball to get hits for two teams, in two cities, on the same day.

Strange things can happen when deuces are wild. Two on, two out, two balls, two strikes. Nothing to lose. Everything to gain. Under what circumstances do you feel you have everything to gain, nothing to lose? § What is your tendency when "Deuces are wild!": do you play it safe or take advantage of the opportunity? § How might you, more often, create those circumstances where you have the sense of everything to gain, nothing to lose?

In his remarkable baseball memoir, *Man in the Crowd*, sportswriter Stanley Cohen waxed lyrical of baseball's box score:

> *Throughout the season, each day is begun with a perusal of the agate type: the results of the previous day's games, the subtle shifts in the standings, the probable pitchers for games to be played that day, and finally, like topping on the cake, box scores, those wondrous blocks of type two inches wide by three deep that relate the individual statistics. Yes, the box score is the catechism of baseball, ready to surrender its truth to the knowing eye. It is all there: the lineups, the batting order, score by innings, the record compiled by each batter, the succession of pitchers, extra base hits and runs batted in, stolen bases and errors, double plays and runners left on base, even the time it took to play the game and the number of people who watched it—all are contained in those splendid little rectangles that, stacked on a page, comprise the history of a day's events.*

But there are, I would add, some details that even the venerable box score can't capture.

BASEBALL AND OUR PILGRIMAGE HOME

On Saturday, September 9th, 1989, Kathy and I carried my parents to The Big A in Anaheim, California, home of the then California Angels. The Angels hosted the Boston Red Sox. Courageous Jim Abbott, born without a right hand, started on the mound for the Angels; outrageous Oil Can Boyd started for the Sox.

We stayed for the entire game.

The starting pitchers both left after five innings.

The box score, with its plentitude of data, reports that Angel outfielder Devon White stole four bases in the game. Ah, but the box score has its secrets; here's the rest of the story on three of Devon's four stole bases:

In the bottom of the sixth—with none out, the Red Sox leading the Angels 5 to 3—Devon White singled to left off Boston reliever Joe Price, scoring Claudell Washington from third. After Chili Davis hit a long fly to center for the first out, Wally Joyner stepped to the plate. With a strike on Joyner, Devon White stole second; two pitches later, he stole third. Joyner lined out to Price for the second out. The Angels' Johnny Ray stepped in. Without warning, Devon White broke from third with Price's first pitch to Ray and stole home to tie the game.

The woman sitting next to me reached down to grab her Coke and missed the play. Hearing the roar of the crowd, she lifted her head and desperately questioned, "What? What happened? What did I miss?"

To put Devon White's accomplishment in perspective, in the history of Major League Baseball, men have stolen second, third, and home in the same inning fifty times. By comparison, there have been 260 no-hitters.

The moral of the story... Sometimes in life, you just have to show up and pay attention. Fully. Now.

THE SIXTH:
CARDS AND GIANTS

Little Leaguers dream of having their own Topps baseball card.
But, regardless of your field, would you really like your professional performance
—your weaknesses and strengths, your failures and successes—
printed on a piece of cardboard and distributed with a piece of bubble gum?

Michael Fox

THE SIXTH:
CARDS AND GIANTS

Collecting baseball cards as a boy was more than a hobby; it was something of a series of rituals, or practices, with its own liturgical calendar of days. In my early years, The Topps Company of New York was the exclusive manufacturer of baseball cards. Beginning during spring training, every six weeks or so, Topps would issue north of 100 player cards, publishing the final group of their annual set in September just in time for the World Series. The gradual release of the set throughout the baseball season held the interest and emptied the pockets of me and my friends and countless others through the Fall Classic. The release of each group of cards was something of a feast day on our calendars.

Baseball cards, with their photos, statistics, biographies, and historical references, were my introduction to and my education in the game itself. But, cards were difficult to find in the stores of my hometown, Lynwood, a suburb of Los Angeles.

One day, however, while still in my single digits or just beyond, I walked to the grocery store for my mother. To my delight, a small, vintage vending machine had been placed—sometime since my last visit—just inside the doors of the market. The mysterious, mechanical stranger offered five baseball cards for a nickel. I withdrew two nickels from my pocket and warily placed them in the lap of two metal protrusions at the front of the machine. I pushed the nickels into the machine and heard the coins drop, followed by a mechanical grunt or two, and watched in wonder as the machine slowly—and with extraordinary effort, it seemed—pushed a small stack of cards through two narrow slots.

The cards were not wrapped in a wax pack, as was typical. Indeed, there was no wrapper; there was no bubblegum; there were just the cards—in pristine condition. And, oh, the cards. They were not cards from the current baseball season; they were not even cards of a recent season. One slot dispensed cards from the Topps 1968 issue. The other slot offered cards from Topps' former rival, The Fleer Corporation of Philadelphia—from a series of cards depicting Hall of Fame players and published in, wait for it, 1962!

I felt like I had paid a nickel and been transported back in time.

I made my purchase for my mother, ran home, and retrieved every nickel I could find. I grabbed an empty box, and raced back to the store. For the next several weeks, while the machine remained in the market, I spent every available nickel on its cards. I emptied the contraption every few days, a nickel at a time. The employees of the store grew accustomed to my presence, but watched with suspicion as I tied up the wondrous time machine and retrieved my treasures.

Sadly, just as quickly and magically as the machine appeared, it vanished. I was heartbroken, but its treasures remain.

I'm curious, have you ever inadvertently stumbled across an unanticipated opportunity—in life, love, or labor? Or, even in small squares of cardboard? § If you are a follower of Christ, have you ever sensed a moment of provendipity, when a door opened unexpectedly? § How did you respond? § What resources did you bring to bear? § What fears threatened the opportunity? § Were you thwarted by your fear? Did you somehow dispel your fear and move forward? Or did you acknowledge your fear and proceed in spite of it? § What's the learning for what's next? § And, what is next? What opportunity now awaits your courage? § How might you summon your courage, your faithfulness, and proceed? § What needs to be done first? § Seriously, why so many questions?

SAFE AT HOME!

Ah, vintage baseball cards

Pieces of old cardboard

Collected as a child

Archived as an adult

Some recent additions

Still relatively few

Merely tens of thousands

[I'm not obsessed like some]

My trove is personal

Treasured designs, sets, eras

Favored players and teams

No doubles to speak of

Nothing for sale or trade

The past fondly recalled

They're my own Cooperstown

They're all a part of home

Ah, memories of home

Pieces of my story

Collected as a child

Archived as an adult

BASEBALL AND OUR PILGRIMAGE HOME

Following the death of Moses, Joshua led the nomadic nation of Israel across the Jordan River and into Canaan. Over the next thirty years, Israel, forty years removed from Egypt, would conquer and settle in Canaan—a land first promised generations before to the patriarch Abraham, a land "flowing with milk and honey."

The crossing of Israel was as majestic as it was momentous. At Joshua's direction, the priests cautiously stepped into the midst of the raging waters of the Jordan with the ark of the covenant upon their shoulders. The torrent deferred to the presence of the ark; its waters retreated and the riverbed downstream dried up. For the next several hours, Israel—some two to four million men, women and children—trekked past the ark in the midst of the thirsty riverbed and entered the land of promise.

Following the procession and at God's direction, a representative of each of the twelve ancient families of Israel chose a large stone from the dry riverbed. The twelve men bore the stones upon their shoulders and led the priests and the ark of the covenant up the opposite bank of the Jordan. At the very moment when the feet of the priests stepped up from the embankment with the ark, the restrained torrent of water was released and resumed its furious course. That night, Israel camped at Gilgal, and there the twelve stones were set up as a memorial to future generations of the day's remarkable events. Joshua explained:

In the future when your descendants ask their fathers, 'What do these stones mean?' tell them, 'Israel crossed the Jordan on dry ground. For the LORD your God dried up the Jordan before you until you had crossed over...He did this so that all the peoples of the earth might know that the hand of the LORD is powerful...' (Joshua 4:21b–24).

Stones of remembrance.

• • •

But enough about Israel, let me tell you about the Philadelphia Phillies and the Houston Astros.

Don't roll your eyes; it's been weeks since I last mentioned baseball.

Thirty years ago, my life was a self-inflicted mess. It wasn't apparent to many, but I was profoundly disengaged with my values and convictions. (Oh, that I may be as gracious with my words toward other prodigals!) And I was in denial. The details are unimportant; in fact, I've spent the past thirty years distancing myself from the details.

But one evening in early autumn of 1980, I casually flipped on the television. One of the networks, to my surprise, was broadcasting a baseball game. A National League Championship baseball game. A National League Championship baseball game—to my greater surprise—featuring the Phillies and the Astros. How could an entire season of baseball—in any other year the baseball season is my own liturgical calendar—have come and gone without my awareness? It's difficult for me to express the sense of desperation I felt at that moment; it was as if I awakened from a stupor to discover I was suddenly alone, far away from home, unable to get my bearings.

Baseball and its historic legacy, Cooperstown, was then—and remains to this day—a stone of remembrance that beckoned me return to the safety of home—to reconcile with my values and convictions.

Writer John Thorn beautifully expressed baseball's power to stir my consciousness when nothing else could:

> *This great game opens a portal onto our past, both real and imagined, comforting us with intimations of immortality and primordial bliss. But it also holds up a mirror, showing us as we are. And sometimes baseball even serves as a beacon, revealing a path through the wilderness* (Baseball: An Illustrated History, p. 58).

Stones of remembrance.

Do you have a stone of remembrance… someone, somewhere, something, that has the power to awaken your values and convictions? Perhaps you have more than one. § Following that "aha!" moment in the autumn of 1980, I visited my parents' home and retrieved my childhood collection of tens of thousands of baseball cards. I had abandoned them to the elements. I restored them to their former place of honor; I restored these stones of remembrance. What stones of remembrance are patiently awaiting your renewed respect? § The Ark of the Covenant was God's own version of Cooperstown, baseball's Hall of Fame. Within that hallowed ark was kept the tablets of stone engraved with the Decalogue, Aaron's staff that blossomed, and a pot of manna. What would it look like for you to craft your own ark of the covenant... a box containing symbols, reminders, of a covenant you might make with yourself, your God, your neighbor?

There's an old photo of Jackie Robinson of the Brooklyn Dodgers stealing home. It's the eighth inning of the first game of the 1955 World Series against the Yankees. Imagine Robinson's girth, his gaze, his grit: he looks more like a locomotive leaving the station than a sprinter leaving the block. He's risking he can move his 205-pound body ninety feet from third base to home plate faster than the pitcher can throw a five-ounce baseball sixty feet, six inches. He would be ruled safe, a call legendary Yankee catcher Yogi Berra would argue to his dying day.

There's a classic photo of Ty Cobb of the Detroit Tigers stealing third. It's a Saturday afternoon in 1909 at Manhattan's Hilltop Park, early home to the Highlanders, precursor to the Yankees. Cobb hurls himself into third base: teeth clenched, eyes determined, spikes flying. Legendary photographer Charles Conlon—reflexively and, indeed, unknowingly—snapped the photograph, one of the most enduring images in baseball history. Highlander third baseman Jimmy Austin—airborne with his back to the camera—on the strength of this photograph, is said to have had the most famous keister in the long history of the game.

And, there's a photo of Sandy Koufax of the Los Angeles Dodgers on the mound of Dodger Stadium. He's hurling his trademark fastball against a player from the Milwaukee Braves. Imagine the painful, distorted contortion of his face; the long, low reach of his frame; the catapult-like motion of his arm. He repeated this motion in the neighborhood of one hundred times each nine-inning contest, over the course of a career in which he started 314 games. Pitching is said be one of the most unnatural motions demanded by any sport; Koufax's intensity exaggerated pitching's toll on his body. Warned by doctors that he was in danger of losing the use of his left arm, he abruptly retired in 1966 after just ten seasons in the Majors.

Robinson, Cobb, and Koufax all played the game with passion as if they had something to prove. If you're curious, read a bit on all three to discover any commonality, any connections.

What or who or where makes your face contort with the sort of tenacity you might imagine on the faces of these men? What good thing calls forth tenacity in you? § What practical things do you do to maintain your tenacity? § Who or what typically threatens your tenacity? What can you do to counter the influence? § But then there's this. How do you keep tenacity from transforming you into a self-absorbed jerk?

I have two dozen baseballs in our living room. No, they're not piled in an equipment bag, on their way from or to the car. I have two dozen baseballs *on display* in our living room.

A third of them form a wreath with a bow—a collection of nondescript game balls knit together into a sense of home. In a hutch across the room, there's an unsigned game ball from a chilly spring evening when we visited Chicago's Wrigley Field before the ivy had awakened to adorn the outfield walls. The balance of the twenty-four balls, also in the hutch, bear signatures.

Most of them, as you might imagine, by baseball players.

It's an odd assortment of players, scarcely meaningful to others. There are baseballs signed by childhood heroes including Willie Mays, Duke Snider, Red Schoendienst, Del Crandall. There's a ball from years ago signed by the entire team of the Texas Rangers—sans budding prima donna Alex Rodriguez. There's a curious ball signed by three relatively obscure pitchers who pitched the final games in the Brooklyn Dodgers' Ebbets Field (1957), the New York Giants' Polo Grounds (1957), and old, old, Yankee Stadium (1973), prior to its extensive refurbishing.

There's one baseball signed by a former quarterback—yes, football—of the UCLA Bruins, Mark Harmon. He's known to a younger generation for his alter ego, the Very Special Agent Leroy Jethro Gibbs.

The remaining baseballs are signed by favorite Christian authors: Ruth Haley-Barton, Robert Mulholland, and N.T. Wright. Mr. Wright graciously signed the baseball with a chuckle, saying, "I've never done this before." Rest assured, if I ever need to speak with him again, I know how to identify myself.

There are two or three contemporary writers I'd yet like to add to my collection. And, there are two deceased authors whose signatures I would love to have on the sweet spot of a baseball: C.S. Lewis and the Apostle John. I once found a baseball signed by the beloved apostle for sale on eBay, but it lacked a Certificate of Authenticity. You have to be careful; there are a lot of fraudulent signatures on the memorabilia market. Besides, John's signature was on a Bowie Kuhn ball, who was Commissioner of Major League Baseball from 1969 through 1984. Call it a hunch, but I passed on the opportunity.

What's the value of my autographed baseballs and other collectibles? Well, beyond knowing. Their worth to me cannot be counted in dollars. They are, instead, evidence that the heroes of my story are real and at home in my world. And they've stopped by and signed my guestbook.

Who would you like to meet—living or dead—and why? § What would you ask them? § What small physical structure—like an autograph—might be a meaningful container to hold that memory?

SAFE AT HOME!

No one could find Napoleon "Nap" LaJoie (Lash-you-way) in 1933. He was supposed to be right there between Bernie Friberg and Heinie Manush. The nation's children even invested their bubblegum money in the desperate search for LaJoie.

But he was nowhere to be found.

Nap LaJoie played second base from 1896 to 1916 for the Philadelphia Phillies, the Philadelphia Athletics, and the Cleveland Naps (named in his honor; today's Indians). LaJoie, beloved among players and fans alike, was inducted into the National Baseball Hall of Fame in Cooperstown, New York in 1937. He was—according to his Hall of Fame plaque—the "most graceful and effective second baseman of his era." LaJoie is regarded as one of the greatest batsmen and among the fiercest competitors in the history of Major League Baseball.

But in 1933, no one could find Nap LaJoie.

Well, his baseball card, that is.

In 1933, the Goudey Gum Company became the nation's first manufacturer to package baseball cards with its bubblegum. Prior to 1933, baseball cards were more likely to be distributed by tobacco companies to promote their cigarettes. Goudey's 1933 set of cards, known as the "Big League Chewing Gum" set, featured 240 cards of current players and former greats of the game. Well, in reality, it included 239 cards of current players and former greats of the game. Because card number 106 was missing. Nap LaJoie.

BASEBALL AND OUR PILGRIMAGE HOME

Although Enos Goudey never acknowledged the strategy, historians believe card number 106 was never designed nor printed—with intention. Frustrated children who sought to complete their sets of cards bought package after package of bubblegum—in the midst of the depression, no less—in pursuit of the elusive prize. It was Goudey's version of a snipe hunt.

The missing card was a marketing ploy designed to sell more gum.

Ingenious. In an icky sort of way.

Goudey made a fortune in 1933, pennies at a time, on the human propensity for completion. To collect or possess all of them. Whatever "them" might be. Maybe baseball cards or cars or emotions or experiences or wins or even people. The implication is that when our collection is complete, we will be complete. Satisfied. Full. But the truth is, we never run out of things to buy, to trade, to collect, to hoard, to taste, to feel. It's exhausting. And it sorta feels, well, like, idolatry.

What, or who, is card number 106 in your life? § What are you thinking of when you reflect, "Hmm. if only I had what she has, I would be complete." Are you certain? What's a deeper truth?

SAFE AT HOME!

THE SEVENTH:
STITCHES

If you don't succeed at first, try pitching.

Jack Harshman

THE SEVENTH:
STITCHES

At the risk of sounding morbid, the death of winter is about to surrender to the life of spring, nature's annual reminder of mortality and immortality, of death and resurrection. And, on countless playing fields across the country—from Little Leagues to the Majors—bats and balls and gloves will be coerced from hibernation. The umpires' shouts of, "Play ball"—baseball's version of Jesus' call to Lazarus, "Come forth!"—will be heard.

And life will begin anew.

I get that this is random, but the number three, a number grounded in the divine, looms large in baseball. There are three bases, three strikes, three outs, three types of anabolic steroids, three sets of three innings for a total of nine, and nine players on the field. Babe Ruth, the most dominant figure in the history of baseball, even happened to wear the number three across the broad expanse of his jersey.

Perhaps the most prominent of baseball's "nines" was the 1927 New York Yankees' lineup; the first six of whom—Combs, Koenig, Ruth, Gehrig, Meusel, and Lazzeri—were affectionately called "Murderers' Row." Four of the six would later be enshrined in Cooperstown's Baseball Hall of Fame.

Curiously, my mind drifts to another team of nines, every bit as formidable as the '27 Yankees. It included nine women: Clio, Thalia, Erato, Euterpe, Polyhymnia, Calliope, Terpsichore, Urania, Melpomene. None of them could hit a fastball; though they could all fool you with their curves. They were the playful Muses of Greek mythology, offering favored mortals both knowledge and inspiration in literature, science, and the arts—all things creative. From the Muses, we learn an important lesson:

Creativity is the result of making unlikely, unexpected connections.

(Think George De Mestral who, while picking cockleburs from his dog's fur, invented Velcro.)

Although most of us have put aside the mythological gods and goddesses of the ancient Greeks, the Muses are alive in our vocabulary. You muse; you are amused. You browse museums; you visit amusement parks. And there's an invitation within these words. When you become stuck in your musing, seek amusement. Leave the museum, and get to an amusement park. Fast. Seriously, don't take yourself so seriously. And, you might just learn another important lesson from the Muses:

Humor is the result of making unlikely, unexpected connections.

(Think Julie Andrews running through a building singing, "The halls are alive with the sound of Muzak...")

Ooh. Creativity and humor flow from the same, well, spring (a spring of water, not the season of Opening Day). Both are the result of making unlikely, unexpected connections. So, the next time you're stuck, get a little silly. Absurd, even. You might just get unstuck.

And life will begin anew.

No clue on how Murderer's Row and the Muses might fare on Opening Day. Strength vs. Creativity. Personally, I wouldn't bet against the Muses.

What shows up in you when you get stuck creatively? Do you hunker down? Or do you lighten up? § So you don't think of yourself as creative? Consider how creativity might be just another term for "problem solving." Have you ever have had occasion to solve difficult problems? § What are your thoughts knowing that creativity and humor flow from the same spring? § What comes up for you when you think of unlikely, unexpected connections? § How might you forward and deepen your learning beyond your current discipline and interest? How might a broader base of knowing help you forge unlikely, unexpected connections? Who would you have to be to become more observant? Where will you begin?

SAFE AT HOME!

There have been some men of great character make their living as pitchers in Major League Baseball: Christy Matthewson, Walter Johnson, Sandy Koufax, Tommy John, Dave Dravecky, Clayton Kershaw, are among my favorites. But, more than men of character, a number of colorful characters have occupied the mound as well: Dizzy Dean, Preacher Roe, Early Wynn, Satchel Paige, Ryne Duren, Don Drysdale, and many more.

Drysdale was a pitcher for the Brooklyn/Los Angeles Dodgers from 1956 through 1969. Drysdale, a Southern California native, was a veritable poster child for California's first Major League team, returning to Los Angeles when the Dodgers moved west from Brooklyn; he was strong and handsome—an attractive personality, but a fierce competitor—equally at home on a movie screen and on a baseball diamond.

He had a frame that stood five feet, eighteen inches tall; he pitched from a mound that added another ten inches to his height; he released the ball as his follow-through swept him toward the batter; his fastball was clocked as high as 100 mph, and he was not shy about using it to brush back, knock down, or knock silly the occasional batter who offended him. Imagine how unnerving it must have been to place your feet in the batter's box against Don Drysdale.

And that's just the way Drysdale and most Major League pitchers prefer it. They rely on intimidation to supplement their natural talent and developed skill.

BASEBALL AND OUR PILGRIMAGE HOME

The legendary Willie Mays once stepped into the batter's box and—forgetting for the moment who was waiting on him sixty feet, six inches away—used his cleats to dig out a backstop for his heel, as was his custom. Suddenly remembering that Drysdale was on the mound, knowing that Number 53 considered the batter's box his personal office space, the superstar—without looking up—reversed course... Mays feverishly worked to fill the hole back in. It was too late. Drysdale's first pitch put Mays on his back. And the second one, too, if memory serves correctly.

Another story—there are many—deserves a mention. One day in the long ago at Dodger Stadium, Cardinal catcher Gene Oliver belted an impressive home run off Drysdale. Before embarking on a slow victory lap around the bases, Oliver committed what was—at least in Drysdale's Book of Common Screed—a cardinal sin: he stood at home plate and admired the ball as it took flight over the fence, effectively "showing up" Drysdale. Then, before rounding the bases, he yelled into the dugout, loud enough for Drysdale to hear, "Hey batboy, come get the bat." The next time Oliver came up to bat, Drysdale, to no one's surprise, planted a fastball in the catcher's ribs. Oliver dropped his bat and fell to the ground, writhing in pain. As the Cardinal trainer tended to the fallen batter, Drysdale yelled from the mound to the Cardinal dugout for all to hear: "Hey, batboy, come get the catcher."

Pitchers have certainly made an art of bending the rules to give themselves an advantage. In addition to the brush back and knock down pitches, there's the enduring use of the spit ball and the cut ball. Other position players have their own wiles: the trapped ball, the hidden ball trick, stealing signs, and more. Even home groundskeepers are known to get in on the mischief: if a visiting team has a base runner who's a threat to steal, the thief may find that the infield dirt extending out from first base has been watered, heavily, prior to the evening's game.

It's a curious thing for a proud competitor to employ deception and manipulation in a contest; for it's essentially an admission that his abilities and drive are insufficient to give him the edge. When the businessperson or client, the scholar or student, the pastor or church member, the prosecution or defense, the Republicans or Democrats resort to the deception and manipulation of circumstances, or people, or truth itself, it's a telling declaration that truth and talent are not on their roster.

Where might manipulation or deceit betray a felt weakness in your character, your convictions, or your curveball?

Charles Dillon Stengel—nicknamed Casey, a nod to his hometown, Kansas City, and to a poem that debuted in his youth, Casey at the Bat—spent sixty years playing, coaching, and managing in the big leagues. His greatest success came as a manager. Of the New York Yankees' twenty-seven championships, Stengel won seven.

Stengel's the only man in history to have worn the uniforms of all four New York baseball clubs: Dodgers, Giants, Yankees, and Mets. From 1962 through 1965, Stengel managed the expansion Mets—their uniforms nostalgically meshing the colors of the fugitive Dodgers and Giants. Their ineptitude (40 wins against 120 losses in 1962) is said to have prompted Casey to exclaim in frustration, "Can't anybody here play this game?"

Nearly a half-century ago, on a Sunday afternoon at Dodgers Stadium, I recognized Stengel's weathered face as he walked toward me in a virtually empty concourse. Walking alongside Casey was Babe Herman, Casey's former Brooklyn Dodgers teammate—both men dressed in suit and tie, their wives following closely behind.

Stengel might have been best known for his distinctive, stream-of-consciousness, monologues about all things baseball. He employed his unique dialect, affectionately labeled "Stengelese," to amuse and to confuse. On July 8th, 1958, Major League Baseball had the good sense to dispatch the beloved jester to a congressional committee investigating baseball's antitrust status. For forty-five minutes, Stengel confounded the congressmen, causing one to say, "Mr. Stengel, I am not sure that I made my question clear." To which Stengel replied, "Yes, sir. Well that is all right. I am not sure I am going to answer yours perfectly either."

Witness a few excerpts from his congressional testimony:

SAFE AT HOME!

In his opening statement, Stengel observed:

I had many years that I was not so successful as a ballplayer, as it is a game of skill. And then I was no doubt discharged by baseball in which I had to go back to the minor leagues as a manager, and after being in the minor leagues as a manager, I became a major league manager in several cities and was discharged, we call it "discharged," because there is no question I had to leave...

Asked if baseball might be expanded to include more teams, Stengel replied:

I think every chamber of commerce...would want a major league team, but if I was a chamber of commerce member and I was in a city, I would not want a baseball team to leave the city as too much money is brought into your city even if you have a losing team and great if you have a winning ball team...

Asked, good-naturedly, if New York City would continue to monopolize the world championship, Stengel responded:

Well, I will tell you, I got a little concerned yesterday in the first three innings when I say the three players I had gotten rid of and I said when I lost nine what am I going to do and when I had a couple of my players. I thought so great of that did not do so good up to the sixth inning I was more confused but I finally had to go and call on a young man in Baltimore that we don't own and the Yankees don't own him, and he is going pretty good, and I would actually have to tell you that I think we are more the Greta Garbo type now from success...

BASEBALL AND OUR PILGRIMAGE HOME

Asked why the minor leagues were struggling financially, Stengel answered, obviously still fixated on Greta Garbo:

Do you know why? I will tell you why. I don't think anybody can support minor league ball when they see a great official, it would be just like a great actress or actor had come to town. If Bob Hope had come here or Greta Garbo over there half of them would go see Greta Garbo and half Bob Hope but if you have a very poor baseball team they are not going to watch you until you become great..."

Stengel concluded his testimony. Mickey Mantle was up next.

A senator asked the young superstar, "Mr. Mantle, do you have any observations with reference to the applicability of the antitrust laws to baseball?"

Likely to the delight of some and to the chagrin of others, Mantle flashed his boyish grin and answered, "My views are about the same as Casey's."

Play ball.

In 1958, Major League Baseball was in trouble. Congress threatened legislation to revoke its exemption from Federal antitrust laws. Casey Stengel was chosen by the owners to represent their interests at the congressional hearing. It's easy to misinterpret Stengelese as the ramblings of a bumpkin. But Stengel was an intelligent man. He used words—and lots of them—with intention to entertain, to disarm, and on occasion to obfuscate the issue. § With no intention to reproach Mr. Stengel...Have you ever been conscious of talking around an issue? Have you ever in mid-conversation realized you were using words—and lots of them—because your position seemed indefensible? How would you weigh the benefits and risks of obfuscation over and against the benefits and risks of transparency? What's the learning?

Did you hear about the big league ballplayer who stole first base? That's right. First base. Running from second.

Among my baseball treasures is a pin and a baseball card—both over a century old—featuring the likeness of Herman "Germany" Schaefer. Schaefer may be the only base runner in the history of Major League Baseball to have stolen first base.

It was Friday, August 4th, 1911, the bottom of the ninth inning. Schaefer—who played in the Majors for fifteen seasons with a half-dozen clubs—was on first for the Washington Senators; teammate Clyde Milan was on third, ninety feet away from scoring the winning run.

Schaefer broke with the pitch and stole second. He was hoping to draw a throw from Fred Payne, catcher for the White Sox, allowing Milan to steal home. But Payne was savvy enough to hold on to the ball and to surrender the stolen base. Schaefer, however, was both enterprising and persistent. And, I would add, perfectly willing to play the fool.

He just figured he'd try it again.

BASEBALL AND OUR PILGRIMAGE HOME

He took his lead on the first base side of second—yes, the first base side of second—and once again broke with the pitch, racing back to steal first, sliding into the bag in a cloud of dust.

Moments later, Schaefer broke for second. For a second time. This time, however, Payne fired the ball to his second baseman. Schaefer got his wish and was caught in a rundown. Meanwhile, Milan raced home from third, but was thrown out at the plate to end the inning.

Itwasthisclose.

What's the relevance? The connection?

It's a simple reminder. When your strategy doesn't work out as planned, don't be afraid to retreat to first, and try again.

My wish list for Major League Baseball's Postseason was rather modest.

Above all, I was rooting for the team of my childhood, the Los Angeles Dodgers, though I knew in my heart they exhibited neither the talent nor the passion to win. After they folded to the Mets, I grew intrigued by the prospects of an all-Texas American League Championship Series; then, Houston and Texas were both summarily eliminated. And through it all, I rooted for the Cubs, curious if this might be the year they could escape the shadows of their past.

SAFE AT HOME!

I'm half expecting either the Mets or the Royals to serve me with a restraining order—effectively preventing me from supporting their team in the Series.

I feel a bit like Ben Cartwright of the old Bonanza television show. For fourteen years, the patriarch of the Cartwrights watched helplessly as every girl his boys showed interest in tragically died before the end of the episode. But then Ben himself buried three wives, all in flashback, of course. Sans the ladies, the writers were able to preserve the integrity of the Ponderosa Ranch Boys Club. Even as a child, I remember watching when one of the Cartwright boys would become enamored with a beautiful young woman; I wanted to shout out to the woman on the inside of the television console, "No, don't do it! You're gonna die!" Voice trailing off in desperation.

Just perhaps, with the World Series void of my favorites, I'll settle in and enjoy this wondrous game for what it is. It's a reminder that sometimes our perspective in life can be skewed by self-interest. It might be a nice change of pace just to be present to what unfolds on the field. Even after a century of organized baseball, we still occasionally see something that has never before been witnessed.

Or, at the very least, we can be thankful that the Blue Jays and their dreadful Rogers Centre, aka SkyDome, won't make an appearance in this year's Fall Classic.

THE EIGHTH:
STORYTELLERS

Sandy's fastball was so fast,

some batters would start to swing

as he was on his way to the mound.

Jim Murray

THE EIGHTH:
STORYTELLERS

I grew up in the Los Angeles tangle of freeways and suburbs. The distant sound of cars and trucks on the interstate was the white noise that lulled me to sleep each night. It's a far cry from the tree frogs and cicadas of Louisiana that lately have assumed the role. From LA to LA. The distance between is a great deal further than you might imagine.

Los Angeles was and is, for many, the terminus of dreams. Contractors and speculators. Artists and actors. Realtors and...well...realtors.

Railroad brochures of the early twentieth century encouraged the migration west from across the country. Of my grandparents' generation, very few were native to the Los Angeles basin, or even the state of California. Even as the East Coast beckoned from across the Atlantic the "tired and poor," the West Coast beckoned from across the Plains the industrious who cherished a dream and who carried a bit of seed money in their pockets. My Grandfather Fox, a contractor, made the trek with his young family from Oklahoma in a Nash Touring Car that he'd accepted as partial payment for a business debt. And not much else in his pockets.

This migration west is evident even in the professional sports franchises that have become identified with the city. Only the Los Angeles Angels suggest local roots. The Los Angeles Lakers? There are a few lakes—perhaps ponds—scattered about the city; there are reservoirs to be sure, but somehow I can't imagine "Reservoirs" in script across a basketball jersey.

Then there are the Los Angeles Dodgers. Indeed, what's a Dodger?

Again, the names of these sport franchises reflect their roots prior to their migration west. The Lakers moved long ago from "The Land of Ten Thousand Lakes," Minneapolis, Minnesota. Makes you wonder what celebrities showed up courtside in those days. Garrison Keillor's grandfather?

And the Dodgers? Well, they headed west from Brooklyn at nearly the same time the Lakers moved from Minnesota. In early Brooklyn the streets were congested with trolley cars. Pedestrians crossed the streets in between the trolleys at their own peril. (Think of a real-life version of the perennial video game Frogger.) Brooklyn pedestrians then—at least those who survived—were affectionately called "Trolley Dodgers." Or, Dodgers, for short. The next time you accuse the Dodgers of a pedestrian effort against an opponent, remind yourself of their origins and ask, "Well, what more should I expect from them?"

Similarly, many of us carry marks of our identity that defined us before we metaphorically moved to sunnier climes. What of you? § Are you still wearing a jersey sporting an identity that no longer reflects the values you now cherish? Think of the apostle Paul: "If anyone else has a mind to put confidence in the flesh, I far more...But whatever things were gain to me, those things I have counted as loss for the sake of Christ" (Philippians 3:4–7). § Might your jersey actually define you as others once saw you, as you once saw yourself, employing words of doubt, derision, and shame? Think of the post-Archie Manning, pre-Drew Brees, New Orleans 'aints, whose fans showed up for home games with paper bags over their heads. § Are you wearing a jersey that no longer makes sense? Think Utah Jazz. Or like the Lakers and Dodgers have you powerfully redefined an old identity, your old scripts? § If you could migrate to a new space, cast off old identities, edit your story, and change jerseys, what would it look like?

I grew up in Los Angeles, a child of the 60s. Fortunately, however, I was young enough, naive enough, to be far more interested in Sandy Koufax and Willie Mays than I was in Timothy Leary and Henry Fonda's troubled kids. When I wasn't listening to Vin Scully and Jerry Doggett broadcast Dodgers games on the radio, I was listening to 93

KHJ's "Real Boss Radio" Top-40 and its legendary disc jockeys—talent with colorful handles such as "The Real Don Steele" and "Machine Gun Kelly." Playlists from AM radio featured artists who still tour some fifty years later and whose popularity, in some cases, is greater than their contemporary counterparts.

I had a difficult time as a child understanding the concept of a radio broadcast. I knew enough to know that when Vin and Jerry were calling a Dodgers game, they were at that very moment ensconced in "the catbird seat"—a name that pioneering baseball announcer Red Barber might have used for a stadium's broadcast booth—sharing live their account of a Major League Baseball game. Why should I think any differently when I listened to the chart-topping music featured on 93 KHJ?

Yes (this is so embarrassing...), I imagined a crowded waiting room at the offices of 93 KHJ where the Beatles, the Rolling Stones, the Beach Boys, and others patiently awaited their summons from the disc jockey behind the glass. I imagined Ringo Starr balancing his drum set on his lap, Mick Jagger cross-legged in a plastic chair flipping about his microphone and its cord like a small baton, while Brian Wilson sat in a quiet corner composing another innovative score to share with his family's surf band. I recall thinking musicians had an awfully tough gig to have to repeat this routine at radio stations throughout the city, only to revisit the circuit again every three hours or so. Did they carpool? And, like so may Angelenos, I didn't factor in how it all might work out in cities and horizons beyond my own.

BASEBALL AND OUR PILGRIMAGE HOME

When I was a child, my imagination was too small to think beyond the realities of my little world. I think back upon the many such misconceptions of my childhood when today I contemplate mysteries greater than AM radio: the relationship between eternity and time; the apparent contradiction of divine foreknowledge and human free will; the question, "How much is sufficient?," and whether or not it's even the right question to ask; the practical implications of James' assertion that "mercy triumphs over judgment" (James 2:13); how the actions of one man, Adam, could corrupt God's good creation, while the actions of another man, Jesus, could reconcile God's good creation; what happens to the odd sock that disappears in the dryer.

How might we compare our inability to fathom divine mysteries with a man living in a one-dimensional world who's trying to comprehend life in a three-dimensional world? § What mysteries perplex you? § How do these mysteries affect you? Do they confuse you? Do they frustrate you? Do they cause you to doubt? Or do they merely intrigue your curiosity, perhaps even heighten your awareness? § How might you remain open to mystery while developing a sense of gratitude that God's imagination is bigger than yours?

SAFE AT HOME!

I really love baseball. The guys and the game, and I love the challenge of describing things. The only thing I hate — and I know you have to be realistic and pay the bills in this life—is the loneliness on the road.

Vin Scully

The voice of Vin Scully—the voice of the Los Angeles Dodgers,—is an echo of childhood and home. In fact, Scully's voice literally echoed throughout Dodger Stadium in my youth; for the transistor radio was new and plentiful among the fans in the stands, and they were all tuned in to Scully's broadcast.

I grew up in the shadow of Dodger Stadium. A half-century later and two thousand miles distant, I no longer have a home place; my parents and a younger sibling are gone. But Vin Scully has remained an enduring, faithful presence.

Some thirty-five years ago, work carried me from Los Angeles: first, to Bakersfield; later, north to Auburn; later, to rural Louisiana. Bakersfield is Dodger territory—it was easy to pick up Scully's broadcast in California's southern San Joaquin Valley. But I remember the day we moved to Auburn, just east of Sacramento. As the evening sun fell upon our journey, my spirit fell. I was homesick, feeling blue. Not Dodger blue. Just icky blue. We drove past the state capitol, aglow in the darkness. I turned on the radio seeking distraction. There, to my delight, wafting through the night from a distant Salt Lake City radio station, was the voice of Vin Scully calling the Dodgers game.

BASEBALL AND OUR PILGRIMAGE HOME

I instinctively sighed and felt at home. Safe at home.

After sixty-seven years and nearly ten thousand games—including three perfect games; eighteen no-hitters; fourteen All-Star Games; twenty-five World Series—Vin Scully called his final game yesterday afternoon in San Francisco. When he broadcast his first game, the Dodgers were in Brooklyn, Truman was in the White House, and Major League Baseball games had not yet been televised. With his retirement another voice from my youth has fallen silent.

More than an announcer, Vin Scully has served as the unofficial poet laureate of Major League Baseball for over half its history. His narration has led people of four generations to fall in love with the game. The morning after his final broadcast, I reflect on a sampling of his most greatest calls.

• • •

Brooklyn's first world championship in 1955:

Ladies and gentleman, the Brooklyn Dodgers are the champions of the world!
[Scully immediately fell silent and allowed the ambient noise of the stadium to tell the story—a practice that became a distinctive feature of his greatest calls. Recalling that autumn day in Brooklyn, Sculley later recalled, 'I could not have said another word, or I would have broke down and cried.']

• • •

Don Larsen's World Series perfect game on October 8th, 1956:
[Entering the final frame of the ninth inning, Scully said...]

SAFE AT HOME!

Let's all take a deep breath as we go to the most dramatic ninth inning in the history of baseball. I'm going to sit back, light up, and hope I don't chew the cigarette to pieces. [When Larsen struck out Dale Mitchell to end the game, Scully reported...] *Got him! The greatest game ever pitched in baseball history by Don Larsen, a no-hitter, a perfect game in a World Series. Never in the history of the game has it ever happened in a World Series. Don Larsen pitches a perfect game, retiring twenty-seven Dodgers in a row.*

Sandy Koufax's perfect game on September 9th, 1965. In the ninth inning, Scully reported:

Three times in his sensational career has Sandy Koufax walked out to the mound to pitch a fateful ninth where he turned in a no-hitter. But tonight, September the 9th, nineteen hundred and sixty-five, he made the toughest walk of his career, I'm sure, because through eight innings he has pitched a perfect game...

And you can almost taste the pressure now. Koufax lifted his cap, ran his fingers through his black hair, then pulled the cap back down, fussing at the bill. Krug must feel it too as he backs out, heaves a sigh, took off his helmet, put it back on and steps back up to the plate...It is 9:41 PM on September the 9th... And there's 29,000 people in the ballpark and a million butterflies... Sandy back of the rubber, now toes it. All the boys in the bullpen straining to get a better look as they look through the wire fence in left field...A lot of people in the ballpark now are starting to see the pitches with their hearts...

BASEBALL AND OUR PILGRIMAGE HOME

The time on the scoreboard is 9:44. The date, September the 9th, 1965, and Koufax working on veteran Harvey Kuenn...

You can't blame a man for pushing just a little bit now. Sandy backs off, mops his forehead, runs his left index finger along his forehead, dries it off on his left pants leg. All the while Kuenn just waiting...It is 9:46 PM. Two and two to Harvey Kuenn, one strike away. Sandy into his windup, here's the pitch: Swung on and missed, a perfect game!

[38 seconds of cheering; Scully is—characteristic of him in moments like these—silent.]

On the scoreboard in right field it is 9:46 PM in the City of the Angels, Los Angeles, California. And a crowd of 29,139 just sitting in to see the only pitcher in baseball history to hurl four no-hit, no-run games. He has done it four straight years, and now he caps it: On his fourth no-hitter he made it a perfect game. And Sandy Koufax, whose name will always remind you of strikeouts, did it with a flurry. He struck out the last six consecutive batters. So when he wrote his name in capital letters in the record books, that "K" stands out even more than the O-U-F-A-X.

• • •

Hank Aaron's 715th home run on April 8th, 1974 to best Babe Ruth's record:

It's a high drive into deep left center field. Buckner goes back to the fence...It is gone! [Scully, characteristically, silences himself for a minute to allow the sounds of the moment to wash over his listeners. Then, he continued...] *What a marvelous moment for baseball. What a marvelous moment for Atlanta and the state of Georgia. What a marvelous moment for the country and the world. A black man is getting a standing ovation in the Deep South for breaking a record of an all-time baseball idol. And it is a great moment for all of us, and particularly for Henry Aaron, who was met at home plate, not only by every member of the Braves, but by his father and mother...As Aaron circled the bases, the Dodgers on the infield shook his hand. And that was a memorable moment...And for the first time in a long time, that poker face of Aaron's shows the tremendous strain and relief of what it must have been like to live with for the past several months. It is over.*

• • •

Injured Kirk Gibson's pinch hit home run on October 15th, 1988, to win game one of the World Series:

And look who's coming up...All year long they looked to him to light the fire, and all year long he answered the demands until he was physically unable to start tonight with two bad legs...And, with two out, you talk about a roll of the dice. This is it. If he hits the ball on the ground, I would imagine he'd be running at fifty percent to first base. So the Dodgers are trying to catch lightning right now...High fly ball into right field. She is gone! [Scully is quiet as Gibson circles the bases, and finally declares...] *In a year that has been so improbable, the impossible has happened!*

BASEBALL AND OUR PILGRIMAGE HOME

• • •

Of Wrigley Field in Chicago, for NBC's broadcast of the 1989 National League Championship Series:

She stands alone on the corner of Clark and Addison: this dowager queen, dressed in basic black and pearls, seventy-five years old, proud head held high, and not a hair out of place. Awaiting yet another date with destiny. Another time for Mr. Right. She dreams as old ladies will, of men long ago: Joe Tinker, Johnny Evers, Frank Chance. And of those of recent vintage like her man Ernie, and the Lion [Leo Durocher], and Sweet Billy Williams. And she thinks wistfully of what might have been. And the pain is still fresh and new, and her eyes fill, her lips tremble, and she shakes her head ever so slightly. And then she sighs, pulls her shawl tightly around her frail shoulders and thinks, 'This time, this time, will be better.'

• • •

A random observation on May 17th, 2016, about dirt. Yes, dirt: *You know, looking at Clayton Kershaw's uniform with all the dirt...Back in 1916, the Yankees were playing in the Polo Grounds, and whenever the Washington Senators came to New York to play the Yankees—would you believe?—they brought their own dirt.* [Chuckling] *You're saying, "What?" Yeh, they did! They would bring their own dirt to dry their hands. And they claimed the soil around home plate in the Polo Grounds was trick dirt. Have you ever heard of trick dirt? (...Fastball banged into right field, base hit...) Yeh, to conclude the thought, the Washington Senators, as they were then called, said that instead of drying the moisture on their hands, the* dirt in the Polo Grounds made their hands slippery and the balls and bats harder to handle. How about that! Trick dirt.

Of the greats of the game he has known:
[Of an afternoon, after school, at the age of thirteen, in the upper deck, right field, at New York's Polo Grounds...] *There was a commotion. A lot of people were running over to another area, not too far from where I was. So, being a kid, I went over to see what all the noise was about. And there he was. The way you would imagine him. (One ball, one strike.) There was Babe Ruth. He had a camel coat on, and he had a cap. Not a baseball cap. A cap. And the kids were all around him, wanting his autograph...How good was Stan Musial? He was good enough to take your breath away...He* [Bob Gibson] *pitches as though he's double-parked...* [Roberto] *Clemente could field the ball in New York and throw out a guy in Pennsylvania...He's* [Tom Glavine's...] *like a tailor; a little off here, a little off there, and you're done. Take a seat...Andre Dawson has a bruised knee, and is listed as day-to-day.* [His pause, and then...] *Aren't we all?*

• • •

Translating Colorado Rockies Manager Jim Tracy's tantrum to the umpires on August 6th, 2012:
[When a call on the field was reversed to the detriment of the Rockies, Tracy sprinted on to the field and went toe to toe with the men in blue. Scully, a talented lip reader, interpreted the Rockies manager for a family audience...] '*He caught the*

ball,' Jim said. 'He caught the blinking ball. He caught the darn ball...That is blinking fertilizer.' I'm doing my best to translate. 'You gotta be blinking me. No way. No blinking way. No bloody way.'

• • •

Reflecting on the 10,000th victory in Dodgers franchise history on April 30th, 2014:

It begins in 1890, with a modest group of Brooklyn ballplayers nicknamed the Bridegrooms, and newly married to the National League. With names like Oyster Burns, Pop Corkhill, and Darby O'Brien, these future Trolley Dodgers outscore Boston 7 to 6 on the 21st of April and put a number one in the win column. 124 years, 2,500 miles, and 9,999 wins later, the heart of the franchise beats: beats strongly, beats triumphantly. A team's heritage, deep and rich, never to be forgotten, only to flourish. The victories come—as we hear so often—one at a time, whatever the pace. As many as 105 in 1953; as few as 48 in 1905. Dodger teams have suited up for 19,080 games; run on and off the field for nearly 200,000 innings; stood on the mound and in the batters box for approximately seven million pitches. And, on April 30th, 2014, the odometer turned over a new milestone: ten thousand wins. It's a figure that binds us happily to the teams of Wilbert Robinson and Zach Wheat. To Ebbets Field and the Boys of Summer: Jackie, Campanella, Pee Wee, Furillo, Newk, and Duke. To the GoGo Dodgers of the sixties behind Koufax and Drysdale—willing and [Maury] "Wills-ing," themselves to win—to the legendary infield of the seventies. The arrival of the impossible in 1988. All the way to the Dodgers of today, new aspirants for glory for a franchise that has achieved so much. Ten thousand is a number for all to celebrate: for the players; the leadership; and—perhaps most of all—the fans. Congratulations, and on to the next ten thousand!

• • •

Clayton Kershaw's no-hitter against the Colorado Rockies June 18th, 2014:

[Entering the ninth inning, Scully narrated the unfolding drama...] *Now, if you don't mind, I'm going to sit back and watch it with you...And, there is one out to go. One miserable, measly out...one strike away* [Seeing Kershaw's anxious wife Ellen, in the stands, Scully encouraged...] *Hang in there, Ellen, hang in there...You try to put yourself in Clayton Kershaw's position...Your mouth has to be dry. Your throat has to be dry. ('Oh' and two.) Got 'em. He's done it! Clayton Kershaw has pitched a no-hitter.* [Moments later, when Ellen joined her husband for the celebration on the field, Scully said...] *And when it's all said and done, you escape all the noise, and talk about a dream come true with his wife, Ellen. Big moment in a young life.*

Calling a game late in 2012, as the Dodgers yet again watched their postseason hopes fade, Vin Scully observed:

Fouled away. Just turned the screw a little tighter here in the ninth. What was that great poem? 'Do not go gentle into that good night. Rage, rage against the dying of the light.' Well, that's where we are. So that's the way this game is. You win, you lose; you celebrate and you suffer.

Ah, and yet again, art imitates life.

Blessings to you, Vin Scully. You will be missed. But after serving us for seven decades—enduring the loneliness of broadcast booths and hotel rooms—we wish you the best. May you be safe at home.

October 3rd, 2016

Jack Buck—late broadcasting legend of the St. Louis Cardinals and sporting events beyond the diamond and the archway—may have been the second greatest baseball announcer of my youth. Behind the Dodgers' Vin Scully. With everyone else tied for third.

Buck called the radio broadcast of the 1988 World Series when injured Dodger Kirk Gibson limped to the batter's box to hit a memorable home run and beat the Oakland A's in the ninth inning of Game One. Buck screeched with genuine enthusiasm for the game and declared:

Gibson swings. And a fly ball deep to right! This is gonna be a home run! Unbelievable! A home run for Gibson! And the Dodgers have won the game 5–4! [And with an impulsive flourish Buck cried out...] *I don't believe what I just saw! I don't believe what I just saw!*

Jack Buck could not believe what he had just seen.

Buck's heartfelt, impulsive exclamation raises a question...

• • •

Is seeing, believing? Or, is believing, seeing?

The answer is unequivocally, yes, depending on who you are.

Some rely exclusively upon their five senses. Until they can feel, hear, see, smell, or touch the previously unknown, they cannot, they will not, believe in its reality.

(But then, if you were Jack Buck, you still might not believe it, even though you've seen it.)

Others, however, can sense or see the unseen because—trusting the goodness of God and the witness of scripture—they believe and are confident that, sooner or later, their faith will become sight.

• • •

Is seeing, believing? Or, is believing, seeing?

This very question came up in the Gospels (John 20:19–29). Jesus joined the apostles—sans Thomas—for a meal on the night following the morning of the resurrection. In the days that followed, Thomas listened to his fellows describe their encounter with the risen Jesus. He responded:

> *Unless I see the nail marks in His hands, and put my finger where the nails have been, and put my hand into His side, I will never believe.*

Ah, yes, move Thomas firmly into the "Seeing is believing" camp.

A week after the resurrection, the apostles—Thomas included—were again gathered together for a meal:

BASEBALL AND OUR PILGRIMAGE HOME

Jesus came, the doors having been shut, and stood in their midst and said, "Peace be with you." Then He said to Thomas, "Reach here with your finger, and see My hands; and reach here your hand and put it into My side; and do not be unbelieving, but believing." Thomas answered and said to Him, "My Lord and my God!" Jesus said to him...

"Because you have seen Me, have you believed"?

"Blessed are they who did not see, and yet believed."

Jesus softly rebuked Thomas for his insistence upon seeing before believing; then he conveyed a blessing on on those unable to physically witness his resurrection, but who anticipate, who trust, who believe. It's one thing to see, and believe; it's another to believe, and see.

• • •

So, is seeing, believing? Or, is believing, seeing?

Nobility spreads its wings over all who believe: those of the seeing, believing camp and those of the believing, seeing group. Admittedly, Jesus in his conversation with Thomas seems to toss an "attaboy" to the latter group.

All of which causes me to pause and inquire—and I invite you to join me—What am I looking for? Do I seek evidence to lead me to faith? Or, do I have the faith that gives me eyes to see what others cannot see? You see?

> *You have eyes—can't you see?*
> *You have ears—can't you hear?*
> Jesus (Mark 8:18, NLT)

SAFE AT HOME!

credo ut intelligam

(I believe in order to know)

Augustine of Hippo

You can't rely on your eyes

when your imagination

[read, 'faith']

is out of focus.

Mark Twain

Open the eyes of my heart, Lord

Open the eyes of my heart

I want to see You,

I want to see You.

Michael W. Smith

THE NINTH:
SAFE AT HOME

*Baseball seems to have been invented
solely for the purpose of explaining all other things in life.*

Roger Angell

THE NINTH:

SAFE AT HOME

Okay, I'm going to let some of you in on a little secret. If you've read less than two hundred of my essays, our relationship might not yet be prepared for this next big step toward intimacy. It might be best if you come back after you have a few more columns under your belt.

What? Are you still here? Are you twelve?

Now, those of you who remain, please move in just a little closer. For the sake of privacy. If you're reading the audible version of this piece—meaning, if a family member or friend is reading aloud to you—please adjust the volume down. If you're reading this electronically, please dim the intensity of the screen.

Well, here goes: I really love the ancient, mystic roots of the game of baseball and the history of Major League Baseball.

There, confession is indeed good for the soul.

Now, I know that some of you have been reduced to a heap with that startling declaration. Like an Early Wynn brush back pitch—the man who, when asked if he'd brush back his own mother with a pitch, replied, "Only if she was crowding the plate." Again, those of you who remain, I encourage you to bear with me for the final point: the principles I am so anxious to share with others, that I am willing to risk such vulnerability and transparency.

In spite of my passion for baseball and the relative ease with which I played it as a boy, there was a day in my youth when the game nearly crushed my spirit.

I was far from home, attending a youth function of the church. On Saturday afternoon, there was lunch and a pickup softball game in the park. Two friends who knew me well were appointed captains and began to select among the many players one-by-one, until one was left. Left out. Yikes. I wasn't angry; I was just hurt. And embarrassed.

As the two massive teams separated along the foul lines, I quietly walked—inconspicuously following my own foul line—to my car. The introvert in me sought the solitude of a bookstore to process what was going on inside my head.

The day of introspection among the stacks turned out to be a pivotal, transformative day in my life. As I spent the afternoon walking and praying and sulking—two of three of these disciplines remain in my daily rhythm of solitude and silence to this day—I came to an understanding.

BASEBALL AND OUR PILGRIMAGE HOME

Although I might never be able to control the way people behave toward me, I can control the way I respond toward them.

Since that day on the ball field, I've adopted seven resolutions to guide me whenever I feel the pain of a personal injustice:

One, I can, in the footsteps of the Christ, be reviled, without reviling in return § Two, I know that my failure to forgive another is most often a resistance to surrender my right to retaliate—or, at the very least, my right to hold a grudge § Three, I can—again, after the example of the Christ—entrust myself to him who judges righteously § Four, I choose not to attach labels that either minimize or demonize another person who may hold an opinion that differs from mine. Further, I can speak boldly of my own, deeply-held convictions, and leave judgment to God § Five, my failure to forgive only leads to self-destructive resentment, and empowers the one who has injured me to live rent-free inside my head § Six, My strong emotional response to a perceived offense may speak more of my own brokenness than of the one who has injured me § Seven, I can only, truly, release to God my anger, my hurt, my perceived right to retaliate when I am willing to surrender myself fully to God—with my personal agenda, ambitions, and outcomes. And these resolutions have brought me life and freedom and peace.

SAFE AT HOME!

Home is where my heart is. I'm returning home from a conference in Chicago, a tad homesick. I can't wait until I am...

Safe at home.

Ah, another pesky baseball metaphor. Baseball's home plate—actually referred to as home base in the rulebook—was originally shaped like the other three bases. It was embedded in the ground and positioned with one corner pointed toward the pitcher's mound. Prior to the 1900 season, baseball owners changed the shape of home plate to the now-familiar pentagon. The shape was ostensibly changed to give umpires a better view of the base to distinguish balls and strikes. It appears to have been mere serendipity—or, as I prefer to think of it, provendipity—that the new pentagon resembled a child's silhouette drawing of home.

Safe at home.

Thirty-three years ago nearly to this day—fresh out of school—I moved from southern California to northeastern Louisiana to continue my education. I love Louisiana, and to this day it remains my home away from home. In those years in Louisiana, however, I was homesick. And there was no email for instant messaging or Skype for video conferencing; and long distance phone calls were expensive and reserved for sharing bad news. Snail mail was most often the only practical way to keep in touch with my distant family and friends.

One Thursday evening in March, way back then, I was alone at the home of R.C. and Julie Bee Reed, my hosts in those days. Oh, I was homesick—almost breathlessly so. I summoned my determination and called upon my creativity to deal with my heart's crisis. I sat down in front of the television and began work on a homemade advent-style calendar that would allow me to count down the days until my scheduled return home to California. Ironically, that night in March, my anticipated homecoming was exactly one hundred days away. One hundred days: three digits. Compounded loneliness and desperation.

As I worked on my calendar, *The Waltons* came on television. (I told you it was a long time ago.)

It wasn't long before the evening's episode captured my attention. You see, the family's mother, lovely Olivia Walton, was homesick, devastatingly homesick for her deceased parents and childhood home. I was in awe of the relevance of the episode's storyline to my personal longing for home. Throughout the show, Olivia's sorrow deepened. Neither family nor friends could understand the depth of her emotions. I'm watching and thinking, "That's right! Others don't get it. Just me and Olivia." Olivia even visited the ruins of her childhood home and—her countenance and posture betraying her heartbreaking melancholy—sat in the old tire swing that remained suspended from a large tree since childhood.

By now, I am enthralled. I have convinced myself that God has intruded into CBS's prime time programming to send me a personal message of healing and encouragement. Why, the name of the actress who plays Olivia Walton is Michael Learned. Television's version of venerable "Walton's Mountain" was not in Virginia, but was within view of my house back home in Burbank. Could the providential points of convergence be any more obvious? I moved closer to the television. I put paper and pen down. I reasoned, "I'll wait and see how Olivia deals with her homesickness, and I'll follow her lead. This is perfect!" The episode continued, and the source of Olivia's depression was diagnosed at hour's end by her physician...

Menopause.

Well, that was disappointing. It did, however, make me feel so silly that I laughed at myself for the remainder of the evening. I'm convinced God has a sense of humor.

So back to baseball...This beloved game of mine is all about leaving home, gallantly seeking adventure on the base paths, and ultimately, triumphantly, returning home, reconciled, to the embrace of family. Sometimes, however, the adventure calls for us to spend a little time on the distant Horn of Second Base, longingly, lovingly, anticipating the moment when we once more are...

Safe at home.

What is safe at home for you? What does it look like? § How do you honor home? Or not? § How do you know when you are away from home? § Who would you have to be to come home? § Is there a physical structure in your life—like baseball in mine—that captures or reflects the value of home? How so?

BASEBALL AND OUR PILGRIMAGE HOME

Have you ever realized a life-long dream? Oh, I have. On the first day of May, a Monday, in the year 2000, Kathy and I walked the short distance—down, naturally, Main Street—from our quarters at the Cooper Inn to the National Baseball Hall of Fame and Museum in Cooperstown, New York. On the previous evening, upon our arrival, we watched ESPN's Sunday Night Baseball broadcast. In Cooperstown. Surreal.

The idyllic village of Cooperstown was founded on the shore of Lake Otsego by the father of James Fenimore Cooper—author of *The Last of the Mohicans* and other classics of American literature I haven't read. Cooperstown, more importantly to me, is the mythical—that is to say, not the actual—birthplace of baseball and home to the Hall of Fame.

As we made our way up the walk to the front entrance of the Hall, I was overcome with emotion. (I know, kinda sad, but if you've ever experienced gratitude for a dream fulfilled, you'd get it.) When she saw I was unable to contain my tears,, Kathy left me outside while she went in and purchased our admissions.

After I had a few moments to settle myself and restore my dignity, we reverently walked inside the old brick, church-like edifice, dedicated in 1939. The first exhibit to greet us was a foretaste of the treasures we'd see throughout the day. There was Babe Ruth's familiar, enormous overcoat—the one I'd seen in countless old photographs—and the original contract that sent him from the Boston Red Sox to the New York Yankees.

Henry Frazee, owner of the Sox and a theatrical producer, sold the promising young Ruth for a staggering package of cash and loans worth almost a half-million dollars—a portion of which was used to finance a new stage play, a production that evolved into No, No, Nanette. No, no, you nuts? With the sale of Ruth, Mr. Frazee unknowingly initiated a century-long inferiority complex within the Red Sox community toward the Yankees.

Ruth's overcoat and contract, along with numerous other artifacts, brought life and color to a mythical man whom I had only known from choppy, old black and white newsreels.

Babe Ruth is presumed by many today to have been something of a buffoon with enormous appetites. In reality, however, the man transformed the game of baseball: from a low-scoring game marked by singles and speed and "inside-the-park" homers to a high-scoring power game dominated by towering home runs that the old ball parks could not contain. Ruth's skills altered the complexion and the strategy of the game and even affected the way stadiums were designed and built.

To illustrate, in 1914, Ruth's rookie year, Frank "Home Run" Baker—no, I didn't make up that ironic nickname—led the majors with all of nine home runs. Nine. For those of you who prefer Harry Potter or the National Hockey League over baseball, that's not very many. Over the next decade, Ruth had a propensity for breaking his own escalating records for home runs in a season until he clubbed sixty in 1927, a record that stood for thirty-four years.

By the way, on that magical day in Cooperstown, we saw the bat Ruth used to hit number sixty. It's worth noting, many contemporary ball players would have neither the strength nor the dexterity to swing the heavy piece of lumber with any success.

Between his appetites and gigantic home runs, Babe Ruth's name became an adjective. No, really. It's in the dictionary. When someone does something of enormous proportions, even on occasion outside of sports, their deed is often described as "Ruthian." Now, how cool is that?

That memorable week in New York began at the Hall of Fame and culminated the following Friday night with our first visit to Yankee Stadium in the Bronx, the original park built in 1923 and affectionately known as "The House that Ruth Built." Honestly, it was like sitting in a cathedral.

The trip was Ruthian.

So, if your name became an adjective, what would it mean? § What would you like it to reflect? § How then will you live to make it so?

Please bear patiently with a tad longer essay this week. Sometimes, it takes time to get home.

I long for home and all that it represents, both to a child and to an adult. I understand, however, that for some the recollection of the hearth fire—its inviting warmth and luminance—is quenched by disillusion. And yet, isn't this very disillusion testimony to the innate longing for home deep within the hearts of all?

Bart Giamatti—the late President of Yale University and, strangely enough, Commissioner of Major League Baseball—once reflected upon home:

> *Home is an English word virtually impossible to translate into other tongues. No translation catches the associations, the mixture of memory and longing, the sense of security and autonomy and accessibility, the aroma of inclusiveness, of freedom from wariness, that cling to the word home and are absent from house or even my house. Home is a concept, not a place; it is a state of mind where self-definition starts; it is origins—the mix of time and place and smell and weather wherein one first realizes one is an original, perhaps like others, especially those one loves, but discrete, distinct, not to be copied. Home is where one first learned to be separate and it remains in the mind as the place where reunion, if it ever were to occur, would happen* (Baseball As Narrative, A Great and Glorious Game, pp. 99–100).

Consequently, gratefully, a sense of home is neither confined to the four walls of a house nor to the quality of our familial relationships. Where then might home be found? For the contemplative, a pilgrimage—a journey to a sacred center, perhaps beyond to a distant place or within to a place that is true—can afford a sense of home, a sense of being. T.S. Eliot defined pilgrimage with a memorable verse:

BASEBALL AND OUR PILGRIMAGE HOME

> *We shall not cease from exploration*
> *And the end of all our exploring*
> *Will be to arrive where we started*
> *And know the place for the first time.*

In the spring of 2000, my Kathy and I traveled to New York City to share dinner and a Broadway show with a client. The trip itself—in hindsight, I see—was the first leg of a lifelong pilgrimage to the distant, historic cathedrals of baseball that would ultimately find us in the Elysian Fields of Los Angeles, San Francisco, Chicago, Boston—as well as the Bronx—and others in between. We began the week in New York state with a visit to the National Baseball Hall of Fame in Cooperstown, New York, and spent our final evening watching a ball game pitting Cal Ripken's Baltimore Orioles against the home team at old Yankees Stadium, the House that Ruth Built. Of the village of Cooperstown, mythical home and archive of baseball, historian Christopher Evans observed:

> *Particularly in Cooperstown, you feel close to the game's nineteenth-century roots. The town is not much more than a remote hamlet, set amid small green mountains at the tip of a long, narrow strip of lake. To call it otherworldly, out of time, Brigadoonish might seem extreme—except to anyone who has been there in summer. Then it would be almost too obvious to mention. It's a surprise to discover that the town's clocks actually move or that a Coke costs more than a nickel. You expect every local to be a farmer, tavernkeeper, or blacksmith* (Baseball: An Illustrated History, p. 61).

The Hall of Fame itself, dedicated in 1939, to the casual observer, appears to be an imposing house of worship. Kathy and I approached the large doors of the museum and—much to my embarrassment—I began to quietly weep for the realization of this moment, this opportunity. I handed Kathy my wallet and—while I collected myself outside—Kathy stepped up to the box office in my stead and paid our admission.

I spent the day escorting Kathy among the innumerable artifacts of baseball's glorious past: Babe Ruth's overcoat; Ty Cobb's diary; Lou Gehrig's locker; Cy Young's pick-up truck; Jackie Robinson's uniform; a turnstile from Brooklyn's Ebbets Field; and more. I took Kathy by the arm and, with the excitement of a little boy, led her from one exhibit to another.

I shared with her the stories behind the artifacts: stories that were once just words on the pages of books I devoured in my youth; artifacts within my grasp that confirmed the veracity of those stories. Prior to Cooperstown, my legendary heroes existed only in black and white newsreels; Cooperstown offered evidence of their historical reality.

Kathy and I walked through the tunnel and on to the field of neighboring Abner Doubleday Field, the fabled—that is to say, not the factual—birthplace of baseball. It wasn't difficult to imagine layers of ghostly players from multiple eras, batting the ball, running to first, chasing a fly; men playing a boy's game.

On our pilgrimage to Cooperstown and in the years since, evidence of the authenticity of baseball's historic narrative somehow witnessed of

BASEBALL AND OUR PILGRIMAGE HOME

the historicity of The Divine Narrative of scripture. Two narratives that, like much of great literature, share the theme of coming home, of reconciliation. Two narratives that live beyond the black and white newsreels of my imagination; two narratives that are living and true.

It was like sliding safely home. *Booyah*.

Where might you imagine yourself embarking on a pilgrimage? It can be, again, either beyond to a distant place or within to a place that is true. § Perhaps, unknowingly, you routinely take pilgrimages, but you were hitherto unaware of their significance. Is there a place to which you always return, either real or imagined? § What's the value that keeps beckoning your return to that place? What's there beneath the surface? § How then might you choose to live powerfully and consciously from the place of that "sacred center," or the home, of your soul?

Cooperstown is a personal metaphor of The Divine Narrative,

a story that is larger than my own.

Do you have a metaphor in your life that connects you to a bigger story?

I experienced Cooperstown on that Monday—far from the metropolitan monoliths where today's ball is played—where security, celebrity and a wide swath of foul territory separate fans from players.

Since that memorable day at the Baseball Hall of Fame, I've experienced Cooperstown, beyond the township, when I stood atop The Green Monster of Boston's Fenway Park... when I sat among the Bleacher Creatures in the right field grandstand of New York's old Yankee Stadium... when I witnessed a ball fly over the ivy-clad outfield walls of Chicago's Wrigley Field... when I made pilgrimage to a dozen distant, historic cathedrals of baseball.

I experience Cooperstown in our home among decades of memorabilia. There's a signed copy of Connie Mack's 1950 autobiography, *My 66 Years in Baseball*. Mr. Mack was an institution in the Philadelphia A's dugout—replete in suit and tie and straw hat—for fifty years, managing the club from 1901 through 1950. It would have been difficult to fire Mr. Mack. He owned the team. Also among my treasures is a *1950 Brooklyn Dodger Yearbook* in near-mint condition. The piece is noteworthy for a small article introducing the newest addition to the Dodgers broadcasting team, a young Vin Scully. The page was later autographed by Mr. Scully, still calling the Dodgers' home games after sixty-five years. Together, these two gentleman's careers have spanned the entire history of Major League Baseball, from 1901 through the present.

I experienced Cooperstown on a Sunday evening in October. I hurtled through the darkness of a lonely Mississippi highway, headed toward the Gulf Coast. Of the many small towns I passed through only one held any interest. It's the small town of Bond, Mississippi, former home to, and final resting place of, legendary pitcher and bigger-than-life character Jerome "Dizzy" Dean (active 1930–1947). As a young boy, I passed Mr. Dean as we walked through a quiet concourse of Dodger Stadium. It seems odd, a half-century later and the breadth of the country farther, to once again pass within a whisper. Three days later I stood before the modest headstone of Mr. Dean and his wife of forty-three years. I reflected upon leaving home and coming home.

But Cooperstown shows up metaphorically in another, a most unlikely, place. Baseball's historic narrative of reconciliation—once the mythical subject of black and white newsreels in my imagination, now confirmed by a century of sensory evidence—strengthens my faith in the historicity of the ancient, archetypal story of reconciliation and coming home: The Divine Narrative of scripture.

What's your Cooperstown? Is there something accessible in your world that allows your five senses to metaphorically witness the distant Divine Narrative? Is it transcendent? Is it true? Is it timeless? How will it sustain you in a time of loss? Incidentally, I'm curious…if there was a Cooperstown filled with artifacts from The Divine Narrative of scripture, what would they include?

SAFE AT HOME!

EXTRA INNINGS:
"GOING DEEP!"

A football player returns a kick-off from one goal line to another.

That's 100 yards or 300 feet.

He returns to the bench where the trainer and two coaches

give him oxygen and monitor his condition.

A baseball player hits an inside-the-park home run and runs the circuit.

That's 360 feet.

He returns to the bench and someone tosses him a towel.

Michael Fox

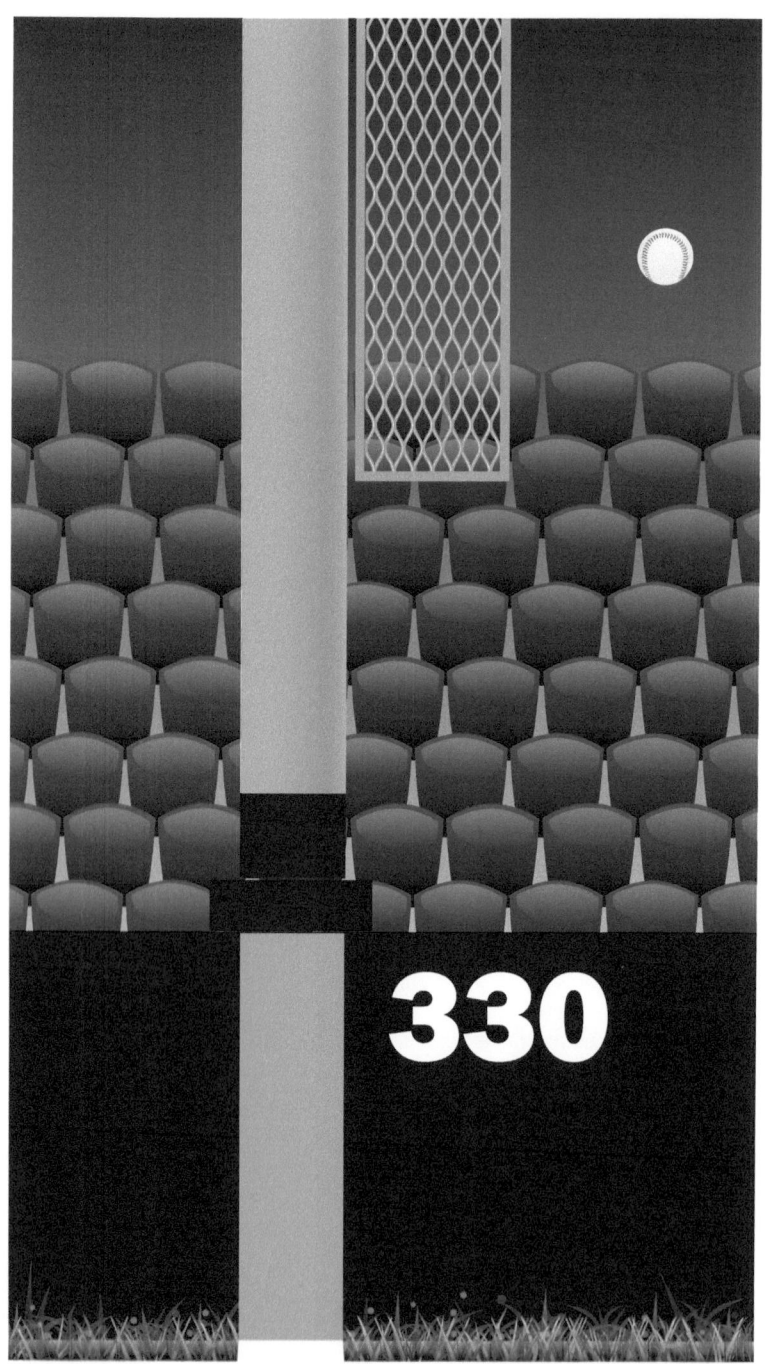

EXTRA INNINGS:
"GOING DEEP!"

I trained as an executive coach under some of the finest coaches in the industry. One day, several seasons ago, I shared the story of my initial visit to Cooperstown with one of my teachers. I explained that my longing to visit Cooperstown was not on my bucket-list. It was on my sippy-cup list. As far back as I can remember, I dreamed of visiting the National Baseball Hall of Fame. I then, somewhat tentatively, shared with my teacher how I wept as Kathy and I approached the museum. As I told him the story, I still could not explain why the Hall of Fame elicited such a profound reaction in the depth of my soul. My teacher, unaware of my longing to understand, blurted, "Hmm, Cooperstown sounds like home."

Oh, the wonders of God.

SAFE AT HOME!

I delight in the wonder of God. But recently I found myself curious about my wonder.

Wonder, you see, has an element of surprise.

If I believe in God and believe him—if I fully trust in his knowledge and power and their gracious offspring, wisdom and goodness—how can he possibly surprise me and fill me with wonder?

Hmm. I wonder...

• • •

I can be surprised and filled with wonder when God outperforms my greatest expectations.

His character and ability are bigger than the measure of our imagination. Scripture is filled with evidence of God outperforming our expectations: the exodus and the cross, the depth and insight of the Word, Jesus, and the word, scripture.

And God still surprises me and fills me with wonder as he continues to routinely outperform my greatest expectations.

• • •

I can be surprised and filled with wonder when God doesn't do things the way I'd expect.

I want a God who is smarter and more capable than me, and who doesn't typically follow my expectations. It's curious, but the prophets of God were particularly aware that God doesn't always do what we expect him to do: I think of the stories—too full to relate in any detail just now—stories of the prophets including Habakkuk, whose prayer received a disturbing reply; Jonah, whose flight from God was canceled, and his return fare booked in the belly of a fish; Paul, whose desire to preach in Rome was granted, though as a prisoner under house-arrest.

And God still surprises me and fills me with wonder as he continues to routinely not do things the way I'd expect.

• • •

I can be surprised and filled with wonder when God doesn't act the way gods are supposed to act.

The God of scripture doesn't behave like the demigods or fictional gods who are always reaching for preeminence. The God of scripture willingly became vulnerable for the sake of relationship and—when that relationship was broken—has relentlessly pursued reconciliation of heaven and earth at a personal cost. He is, as one writer described him, the God of the towel.

And God still surprises me and fills me with wonder as he continues to routinely not act the way gods are supposed to act.

• • •

What might you add to the list? Are there any other ways God surprises you and fills you with you wonder?

My passion for baseball, its history, its Cooperstown was likely inevitable. For the game and its storied past and its artifacts are the metaphorical expression of a hard-wired value in my soul: a value around home and origins and connections.

Here's my invitation to you.

I'd like you to identify the compelling value of your soul. The value, or passion, that defines you, that moves you, that fills you. Then, identify a metaphor that captures the soul of your value. Like baseball, the metaphor that awaits likely already has a presence in your home or office. It may be a small physical token that anyone else would overlook. You, however, have sensed a deep connection with it from the very beginning. Long before you identified your compelling value, your soul recognized it in this object.

It can be quite a process to name your compelling value. Most people need some help (maginecoach@att.net). But here's how you start...

• • •

First, identify three defining moments of your life. A defining moment is unlikely to be a large event: birth, betrothal, or burial. It can be either a pleasant or an unpleasant snapshot or memory. A pleasant, resonant, memory might be of a moment when you felt, "I was born for this!" An unpleasant, dissonant, memory might be of a moment that made onlookers quiver and duck for cover. Either resonant or dissonant, you'll find that a defining moment was a time when your emotional reaction was disproportionate to the actual event that elicited the response.

Choose your defining moments from a broad swath of your years. Don't restrict them to what happened at 3:00 last Thursday afternoon!

Next, give careful, unhurried thought to each of your defining moments. Ask yourself, "Why was this moment resonant, or dissonant?" When you think you've found the answer, ask once again, "Yes, but why?" Like a petulant child, with each subsequent answer, ask once again, "Yes, but why?" Ask, "Why?," at least three times; each time you will force yourself to dig deeper, to uncover greater riches of insight.

• • •

Second, name your favorite books or movies. Choose three or four. If it's a book, you might own the hardcover edition, the expanded paperback, and you keep a copy of the book on your Kindle reader. Just in case. If it's a movie, you may well own the general release version, the director's cut, and the Danish release with Italian subtitles.

Next, consider each of the titles in turn. How does each resonate with you? Is it the genre? The plot? A theme? A character? A scene? It might be anything. Compare your discoveries from one title to the next. You'll likely see a distinctive theme that is common to each title. How would you describe it?

You'll likely discover that the theme shared among your books and movies is folded up in your defining moments, as well. This is your compelling value beginning to show itself.

• • •

SAFE AT HOME!

Third, if you have not yet had insight into your value, consider the themes that occupy your idle thoughts? What do you think about when don't have to think about anything? When you dream with your eyes open, what do you see? It might be helpful to recall your early childhood—when life was not quite as complicated, with less brokenness and fewer burdens. What did you think about? What did you dream about? Who did you pretend to be?

Be aware, it may take time to clarify your defining value, and even longer to find a metaphor that gives depth of expression your passion. But, it's a wondrous journey, a pilgrimage. When you find it, it will feel very much like you've made it.

Safe at home.

BASEBALL AND OUR PILGRIMAGE HOME

SAFE AT HOME!

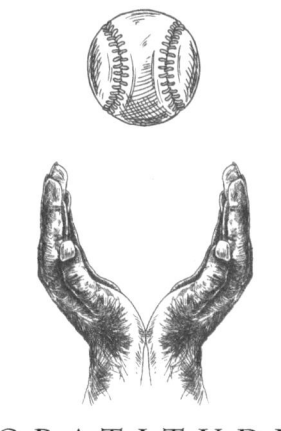

GRATITUDE
Philippians 3:3–5

Breaking the alabaster box for several who have fulfilled my baseball dreams. For my father, for occasional Sunday afternoons at Dodger Stadium, followed by early supper at the Downtown Los Angeles Statler Hotel. For my Kathy, for Cooperstown. For Jim Bobst, for inspiring my baseball pilgrimages. For Don Pruitt for his annual handcrafted Opening Day cards. For Alexis Korbey, for her gift of editing and finding the breadcrumbs. For Sibyl for years of encouragement and direction. For Lydia Richards who first unpacked Cooperstown.

And a special weight of gratitude for Mike Oestmann and John Volke's unforgettable grace throughout 2017's *Best Season Ever Baseball Tour*: Opening Day; an American League Championship game; and, wondrously, Game 3 of the World Series featuring my Dodgers and their Astros. I never would have imagined. I never will forget.

SAFE AT HOME!